Praise for Ken Foster's *The Dogs*

"This book isn't about Foster as much as it's about his dogs, who help him through 9/11, a heart condition that lands him in the hospital, and the deaths of two good friends...Interspersing vignettes on topics such as missing dog posters, shelters, heartworms and understanding dogs' body language, Foster fleshes out this charming account of a life among dogs while providing hints for would-be dog savers."—*Publishers Weekly*

"Ken Foster's new memoir, *The Dogs Who Found Me*, is a tale of love and survival—through 9/11, through a near-fatal heart problem, through Hurricane Katrina...It's a memoir that will appeal to dog-lovers, for sure, but it's also a human story of considerable dimensions, framed by national tragedies..."—*The New Orleans Times–Picayune*

"The reciprocal nature of rescue is the subcurrent to Foster's strange, beautiful and funny account of dog love, dog neglect and the dog-human nexus that fuels both equations. This light, deeply felt chronicle puts that best-selling confection, *Marley & Me*, in the shade. Foster, who lives in New Orleans with at least three dogs, shows readers the moral divide that Hurricane Katrina blew into town."
—*The Cleveland Plain Dealer*

"Foster's book might sound dangerously warm and fuzzy, but it main-tains an edge of wisdom and self-awareness...Foster has led an untidy life, and he's lucky his pets have taught him the value of letting things get messy."—Sarah Goodyear, *Time Out New York*

"(Foster is) matter-of-fact, sometimes angry, always open-hearted and often full of wonder...At the core of it, this is a book about living a de-cent life and taking care along the way. You don't have to rescue stray pit bulls to know how important that is."—*The Oregonian*

"This book is for everyone—not just dog lovers. Foster recounts his doggie and human adventures in a readable, humorous, touching style. The reader can feel his empathy, concern and humanity as he tells of his rescues, his requited love of the dogs he finds, and the wonderful things they have taught him"—*Best Friends Magazine*

"...touching collection of essays and insights..."—*Mississippi Magazine*

Interlibrary Loan
Development Grant, 2008

Other books by Ken Foster:

The KGB Bar Reader (editor)
The Kind I'm Likely to Get
Dog Culture (editor)
The Dogs Who Found Me

dogs I have met

and the people they found

Ken Foster

The Lyons Press
Guilford, Connecticut

An imprint of The Globe Pequot Press

The Lyons Press is an imprint of The Globe Pequot Press

10 9 8 7 6 5 4 3 2 1

Printed in the United States of America

ISBN 978-1-59921-129-9

Library of Congress Cataloging-in-Publication Data is available on file.

For Duque, and the dogs of Costa Rica

contents

House of Dogs **1**

•

Chasing after Duque **7**

•

The Stranger Beside Me **27**

•

Sula's Bad Mood and Her Bad Tummy
and Her Bad Platelets and Her Bad Vet **37**

•

Dogs on Desire Street:
A Dog's-Eye View of the Recovery **49**

•

A Unique Dog **69**

•

The Odd Couples **81**

•

The Vegans in New York **91**

•

Jimmy Is Waiting **103**

•

The Beagle Who Bit Me **117**

•

The Chicago Loop **125**

·

In Dog Years **139**

·

Children and Dogs **149**

·

The Lady and the Tiger **159**

·

The Happy End **165**

·

Resources **177**

house
of dogs

IT'S THE MIDDLE OF THE NIGHT AND I'M SITTING AWAKE listening as my little Sula rattles the house with her snores. I'm not kidding—the old barge-board floor is humming. And then Zephyr joins in, adding her own short nasal bursts in response to Sula's larger, more melodramatic performance. Together, they sound like dueling tubas. Occasionally a foghorn joins them from the Mississippi River a few blocks away. Of the four of us, Brando is the only one who isn't known to snore at all, but that may be because he is able to stretch out comfortably across the bed. Why he is allowed this privilege, before even me, is one of the mysteries of living in a house of dogs. And the crazy thing is that I don't mind at all. Crazy, that is, if you don't have a houseful of dogs yourself.

Last spring, Terry Gross asked me to describe my relationship with Brando when I was a guest on her NPR show, *Fresh Air*. "He's my soul mate," I said, without thinking. I say some of my best things without thinking, but in this case I really hoped that it might be edited out. I wanted to appear at least somewhat rational on the subject of dogs. No such luck.

1

And while I did get a few e-mails from people who accused me of being sick, irresponsible, and wrong, I found far more people who felt the need to write to say, "When you described your dog as your soul mate, I was relieved to know I'm not the only crazy one." (And, just as frequently, "I knew you must have been talking about a pit bull.")

Dogs are the common denominator—unless you are talking with certain cat people, or that rare unfortunate person who has missed out on the amazing lessons to be learned from dogs. Dogs transcend all of the things that keep us from thinking we can understand each other: age, class, race, vocation.

Even geography. When *The Dogs Who Found Me* was published, I discovered that I had an amazing opportunity: While traveling to promote the book, I got to meet hundreds of amazing dogs who introduced me to their equally amazing people. In many cases, the dogs had been rescued, quite literally, from death row, due to perceived health and behavior problems. But in each case, someone decided that they were worth the work of saving.

Before I get started, I have a disclaimer to share: Difficult dogs make more compelling stories. We all know people who have perfect dogs, well mannered, with no issues or health problems. But we're unlikely to hang on every word of that friend sharing the story of how their dog never barks, never vomits or gets diarrhea. There's no drama there. But the value of working with troubled dogs isn't limited to great storytelling. Humans and dogs learn from our challenges and working together to overcome them.

As I type this, my shirt features several blotches of Kaopectate—not from missing my pit bull Sula's mouth, but from the kisses she gave me immediately after receiving this morning's dosage. Brando, the giant brindle Dane/pit mix, is relaxing on the bed after a visit to the vet for his latest Adequan injection; at six and a half, he's been diagnosed with osteoarthritis. These latest ailments are just the tip of the iceberg with these two. If I have a dog who approaches normal at all, it is the rottie mix, Zephyr, who spends her time in the park squirming across the lawn on her back, going from person to person begging for tummy rubs, and then dragging a cloud of dust back to the house with her, like Pigpen from *Peanuts*.

One of the remarkable surprises of doing rescue work—whether it's fostering dogs or volunteering in a shelter—is that each dog stays with you long after they've found their home. These are dogs who may have issues, but their issues, and our growing understanding of what they are about, are part of what bonds us to them. But it isn't just their complex personalities that sear them into our memories; it is also their history of relationships with the people who helped them along the way. It is their small triumphs and the simple fact that dogs don't ever give up.

This past year is bursting with great dogs that I will never forget: the pit bull who raised a piglet as its own; the hemophiliac dog trained as a therapist; the Ninth Ward dogs who returned with their owners to rebuild New Orleans. There were equally memorable people: the owner of a day spa who trained to provide acupuncture to special needs dogs, another novelist who rescued thousands of dogs in memory of his wife's unforgettable retriever and the woman who followed her young daughter to a shelter as her chaperone and stayed to work with dogs on her own.

All of this, some people will say, is not normal . . . whatever normal is. Those people can put this book down right now; I didn't write it for you. I wrote it for the dogs, and their dog-crazy folks. And for Duque, who will never be forgotten.

Hi,

I just heard your interview with Terry Gross on NPR. Then I went to Amazon and ordered your book.

I'm going to attach a picture of my found dog, Emma. She's part pit, part Lab, part I don't know what. Our yellow Lab, River, died on September 10, right after my mom died. We had River for thirteen years. Emma came to us about six months later and was truly a healer. I loved the story about your dog who, after your heart surgery, kept putting his ear against your chest to make sure that your new heart was working. Amazing . . . but I get it. I'm writing to you (something I never do) because I am a potter. My studio is called Muddy Dog Studio, after Emma, who is usually muddy. I would love to send you a dog . . . they are made out of clay. You can see them on my website, www.muddydogstudio.com. But I need an address to send it to.

Thank you for your book and
a great hour on NPR.
Katie

chasing
after duque

IN AUGUST THE TICOS MAKE THEIR ANNUAL PILGRIMAGE
to Cartago to honor La Negrita, the patron saint of Costa
Rica. This year I arrived just a few days late, in time to see
the news coverage in the local papers, declaring the pilgrimage one of the largest in years. It had been six years since I
had lived in Costa Rica at an artists' colony in the village of
Ciudad Colón, and during that time I had visited La Negrita
several times, dragging reluctant Americans with me to the
back of the basilica to see the tokens people left in thanks.
Most of these are in the form of small metal charms repre-
senting whatever prayer had been granted: arms, eyes, legs,
dogs, horses, houses, and also bowling statues, award rib-
bons, wedding photos. You could see the whole country in
that one room.

According to legend, La Negrita—a small black statue of
a girl—was found alongside the river by a girl washing clothes
against the stones. She carried the small figure home, but
when she woke in the morning, it was gone. She returned to

the river, where the statue was once again found. Each time she took the statue home, it reappeared at the riverbed. Finally, she went to the church leaders to tell them, and it was agreed that this was a sign that the bed of the river was blessed and would make a stable foundation for the new church, whose construction had been plagued by earthquakes. The river still runs beneath the church and is considered holy. Even during the off-season, people bring their newborn babies to the water. Teenagers come to brush their teeth in it.

In the year 2000, I lived in Costa Rica for six months and fell in love with the dogs. There were many visitors on the farm during my stay there, and everyone knew about me and my love for Duque, who, like most dogs in Central America, didn't seem to belong to anyone. On my last visit to La Negrita, I put a coin in the box and lit a candle, and the two Americans I was with that day expressed their surprise.

"What are you praying for?" one asked.

"I can't tell you," I said, as if telling her would ruin the prayer and my wish wouldn't come true. The other woman with us said, "I think I know."

I was lighting a candle for Duque, the dog I had to leave behind.

Dogs don't last long in Costa Rica, particularly in the countryside, where even if they are owned, they are allowed to run free, down the unpaved, winding rock roads, into the villages where they hang out on corners waiting for food. In Ciudad Colón, at the one restaurant in town, they would wander in and sit in groups around each table, or, if I was there, climb directly into my lap. Duque lived on the farm at the top of the hill, where I stayed in a small apartment, and he joined me every day for an afternoon nap, and then returned each evening to guard my door. Sometimes, we would play tug-of-war with a sock and then race each other up the damp, mossy-tiled road to the very top of the mountain. This was long before my heart gave way to a pacemaker. This was before 9/11. Before moving south to New Orleans. Before Katrina. My three months in Costa Rica with Duque represent a plateau in my life, the solid ground I can look back on when things get rocky. Yet when it was time to leave Costa Rica, the airline insisted that I leave him behind.

I knew that he wouldn't be there when I returned, which probably had something to do with the length of time it took for me to go back there. That, and Brando, the dog who took Duque's place when I got back to New York and realized that I couldn't live without one. When I finally did return six years later, I prepared myself for Duque's absence as much as I could. I promised myself that I wouldn't expect to see him running up the tiled drive, or burying dog biscuits beneath the bamboo outside my door. And I knew not to ask after him with any of the locals who might still remember me. I knew not to ask because I didn't want to know, and also because I didn't want to reveal that I was still thinking about a dog I had only known for a few months, six years ago. A lifetime, in dog years.

There was a white horse that lived in a small corral on a terraced piece of land halfway down the mountain. I had passed him several times a day, walking down to the village and later walking back up. He always stood in front of his stable and never moved toward me until, after a month of passing him, I went to the Caribbean coast for a few days. Upon my return, I was hiking from the bus stop back up the mountain when I heard the horse whinny before running to the side of the road to greet me, which he continued to do each time I passed by for the remaining two months. But he never let me touch him.

On Christmas Eve, the day before I left, Duque joined me at the horse's gate, and I introduced them. Duque stretched his neck up toward the horse, and the horse bent down until their noses touched, and then they backed away.

Early Christmas morning, as I was leaving after my three-month stay, my cab drove slowly down the unpaved road past the white horse's yard. He saw me through the open window and ran to the edge of the road as the driver continued down the mountain, oblivious to everything I was leaving behind.

Six years later, I walked back to the white horse and stood at his fence, waiting to see if he would come to me. He stared in my direction for a few minutes, tapped his back leg into the ground, and approached me. He came closer than he ever had before, and soon he was running his giant nostrils along the top of my head and face, inhaling and exhaling his horsy smell on top of me.

• • •

Within a few hours of my return, the truth was revealed. I was in the Big House of the property, talking with Francisco and Avery and a new dog named Forest, a chunky chocolate Lab who didn't like to move much.

"You were here when Duque was here," Avery remembered. "He's dead now," he said, and then continued with the details I didn't want to hear. "Someone shot him in the village."

I had rehearsed this moment often enough, so I just managed to nod, as if I had already known. I didn't ask when it had happened, but assumed that it was long enough ago that the emotion of the events had receded into history for Francisco and Avery. For me, all of this information was new—and painful.

"He bit someone," Francisco said.

"No," Avery said. "He bit another dog. Had him by the leg and wouldn't let go."

This wasn't the Duque I remembered, although he wasn't neutered and sometimes got into trouble pursuing the female dogs in town. But when I'd known him, he was well fed, and people played with him. There was no telling what had happened to him after I was gone.

I waited until the conversation drifted to another topic, and then excused myself to my room.

Grief and guilt are necessary but often useless emotions—unless you can channel them into something more. I had returned to Costa Rica to relax and to write, but once again, Duque was leading me somewhere unexpected.

Among the many changes that had taken place in recent years was the fact that the farm was now wired with access to the Internet. I sat in my bed and began Googling terms like *"costa rica dog shelter"* and *"costa rica animal welfare"*; I found two listings within my range: an organization called the McKee Project and the story of a woman named Patricia Artimaña who was running an animal shelter just outside of Ciudad Colón, called the Asociación Arca de Noé. Earlier in the year, the municipality had intervened when neighbors complained about the barking of over one hundred dogs on her property. In the news story, which was now several months old, Patricia said that if she couldn't find homes for the dogs, she would set them free again before she would allow the government to do anything with them. In my short time back, I had already noticed that there were far fewer dogs roaming the village. Now, I understood why.

I e-mailed the McKee Project, introducing myself and explaining that I was a visiting writer who was interested in learning more about their programs while I was in the area. I didn't tell them about Duque. After exchanging e-mails back and forth with Carla Ferrara, we agreed to meet at the Café Vivaldi at the Multiplaza in Escazu. This was a disappointment, as I had hoped I might be able to meet them in their facility, wherever it may be. But they were busy with appointments, and the Multiplaza, one of the largest shopping centers in Central America, was an easy meeting place. We set a date and time to meet.

• • •

On walks around the *finca*, I occasionally ran into Forest, sitting and staring at an orange as if it was a toy someone should play with. But if I threw it for him, he didn't seem that interested in playing chase. He stuck close to his house, most often looking down at the world from his raised patio. He had taken over Duque's job of keeping an eye on everyone, but he preferred doing it from a lounging position.

Thalia was a blond cocker spaniel who ran like a maniac through the property. She was fearless. I was staying in a new building that contained four small apartment units; the terrain was so steep that the jagged edge of the mountain was just a few feet away from where they had created a plateau to build on. One morning I saw Thalia scaling that earthen wall, determined to conquer it. Later, she joined me as I hiked up to the groves at the top of the mountain, where Duque and I had once played with a sock. I didn't offer her any socks; I didn't want to get that involved.

But of course she fascinated me. She could barrel up and down the steep road, disappearing under the brush while I watched from the safety of the paved surface. I tried to remember the physiological experience of running up this mountain six years earlier, but it seemed a distant memory. I had no pacemaker back then. Midway up to the grove there was a flat resting spot off to one side, with a clear view down to the village below. You could see the steeple of the church, the soccer field across from what had been the village market, now converted into an outdoor performance space. Thalia sat looking out over her town, and I remembered Duque doing the same, and how I'd wondered at the fact that one never hears about dogs getting too close to the edge and falling to their death. I have a fear of heights and have to stay back to avoid vertigo. A wide paved road divided the mountain in the distance across from us. I followed it with my eye to see two new, palatial residences at the mountain's crest. We were surrounded by changes.

• • •

The last time I had been to the Multiplaza I had watched from the bus as motorists swerved to avoid a bull that was strolling casually down the middle of the eight lanes. They were used to it; stray livestock on the highway is a fairly common sight in Costa Rica. The bull had turned and wandered into the parking lot. I imagined he was doing some last-minute holiday shopping.

Now, Carla Ferrara and I sat at a small table in the midst of the busy, artificial environment of the mall, surrounded by designer boutiques selling expensive clothing with North American names, even though they'd been manufactured outside the U.S.—in some cases in Central America—for cheap. We split a fruit tart as Carla shared information and brochures on McKee.

"We don't believe in sheltering animals," she said. There were just too many animals, and too few places for them to find homes. You ended up with overcrowded shelters while the problem of strays continued in the streets. The money spent on long-term care, they had decided, would be better spent neutering the stray populations.

"But I heard that there *is* a shelter, somewhere near Ciudad Colón?" I asked.

She seemed cautious when answering this query. "Yes, I know the woman you are talking about." She paged through a copy of *Pets Y Más*, a bilingual animal care magazine that is distributed throughout the country. "Here she is," she said, pointing to a story on the Asociación Arca de Noé. "And here is her phone number. It might be interesting for you to visit. She uses the dog waste to make methane."

I thought perhaps I had misheard, but chose not to question it. Carla continued explaining the McKee Project's mission: They had been training vets across the country to perform spay and neuter surgeries using a tiny incision. The surgery can be performed in as little as ten minutes, giving one vet the ability to carry out the procedure on dozens of animals in a single day. The recovery time is quick for the animals as well. After providing this free training, they then encourage the vets to offer the surgery for free in their villages on a designated day each month.

"They were reluctant at first," Carla said, "but they soon found that people who had never brought their pets in for treatment before came back again for other services. So it was good for business."

As I listened, I once again wondered if I was misunderstanding something. If it was possible to spay and neuter animals so quickly, why had I never heard of this process before? When my own Sula was spayed, the procedure had required overnight observation and had cost an arm and a leg. Wouldn't this new procedure be just as valuable in the States? But these were not questions Carla could answer for me.

"So, you spay and neuter and then put them back on the streets?"

"Yes," she answered, aware that this idea would seem truly foreign to me. Part of the problem is how you define the term *stray*. Studies suggest that only 5 percent of the Costa Rican dog population is truly stray; the rest have feeders, owners, and places to stay at night, but run free throughout the day. Only 25 percent are sterilized, which was actually accomplished in just the past six years.

"If we can get to 70 percent of the population, then we will have the overpopulation under control," said Carla. Previously, the government solution had been to poison animals in the street. McKee has worked to make that practice illegal. They also passed legislation making it illegal to sell animals in parking lots, such as the one outside the Multiplaza.

"Do you remember how people used to sit outside with boxes of puppies?" she asked. I did. I also remembered seeing a man trying to sell a goat at Christmas in the pedestrian mall in San José.

Carla's manner was sharp and efficient. She didn't let her emotions get in the way, even when I finally told her what it was that had inspired me to contact her—the story of Duque and the way he was killed.

● ● ●

I first met Patricia Artimaña in a small bakery across from the church in Ciudad Colón. It was raining outside, the typical evening deluge of the rainy season, and we were sitting with a view of the typical town square. The Ticos love to show off things that are typical. She wasn't a Tico; rather, she was French, but had lived most of her life in Central America. There was a resulting mix of languages that made everything a little more uncertain for both of us. She told me about the municipality intervening earlier in the year, when she had over a hundred dogs.

"I had too many," she said, and I wondered if she really believed that, or was simply repeating what she had been told.

"How many do you have now?" I asked.

She thought for a while and then made a number using the fingers on her hands. Eighteen. "Do you want to meet them?" she asked.

We made a plan for the next morning: A cabbie friend of hers would pick me up on my mountain and drive me to hers, one called Piedras Negras. On a map, it appears to be just outside of town, but maps don't take into account the steep terrain and the winding roads. Over an hour later, we arrived at her house. I had no idea where we were. And, of course, I had fantasies of finding Duque frolicking among the other dogs when we arrived. I knew that this wouldn't happen, but I couldn't expel the image from my mind.

Just a dozen or so dogs appeared at the gate immediately, yet I could see there were more. The property was set up with a series of corrals, with different groups of dogs in each area, some allowed to run completely free. At the top of the property was a stall with several horses, an ox, a flock of geese, and some small, indigenous tree animal that was hibernating in his coop and wouldn't come out to see me. In order to get to the house, I needed to enter the corral, but the dogs weren't about to let me. At each gate the dogs would gather, jumping and barking at me, anticipating my visit. Finally she pointed to another entrance.

"Would you mind coming through here?" she asked. It was a dog door, but it seemed to be the only door that the dogs had no interest in. I ducked down and crawled through.

In the house, more dogs were waiting for us. On the kitchen table, three dogs sat wagging their tails. They were not small dogs, each one weighing at least forty or fifty pounds. Old wooden furniture was scattered through each room, and after a moment (as if my eyes had to adjust to this new world), I recognized that the furniture had once been upholstered, but had long ago been stripped down to the frame. There was no mistaking it: the house was theirs.

On the stove, two large pots of dog food were being slow-cooked over a gas flame. A plastic tube ran from the back of the stove through the wall and across part of the lawn, to a plastic fermentation tent. She was, indeed, turning the dog poop into gas for the stove.

"How many dogs do you have?" I asked.

Patricia thought about it again. "Fifty-five." She wiped down the table and pulled out a chair for me to sit down. Then she went to the stove to make coffee. I scanned the shelves of an open cupboard, lined with various medicines and treatments that I assumed were for the dogs. While the coffee brewed, she introduced me to more dogs. They each had names, but it was more than I could do to keep up with them. A small brown dog made her way through the pack to greet Patricia, then settled at her feet, looking up at her with stubborn longing.

"Oh, Julie," Patricia said. "Poor Julie." She turned to me. "This is a special dog. This is a dog I found myself. I kept an eye on her, brought her food. Eventually she let me take her home." Julie climbed into Patricia's lap and stayed there as the other dogs voiced their disapproval, and eventually Patricia put her down with the rest of the dogs again.

Patricia continued to introduce me to the dogs, and my fantasy that Duque would appear, miraculously alive, dwindled. As we walked onto a patio area, a huge, long-haired, rust-colored dog bounded toward me and rose on his back legs to butt his chest (his brisket) against mine. He came back to me several times during my visit.

"He likes you," Patricia said. "Maybe you can take him home."

I thought about what Carla had said—that sheltering dogs was a waste of resources, that it simply displaced the problem, while few animals actually found homes.

"Will any of these dogs be adopted?" I asked. Patricia shook her head no.

"They are too old. We have other young dogs who can find homes. They don't stay here. Those we adopt—we have adoption fairs." Adoption fair—such a strange North American term.

As we sat drinking coffee, Patricia lifted the cuff of her pants to show me that she had a wound, a bite at her ankle. She explained that it had become infected; one of the bottles of medication was her own antibiotic. "I was on vacation," she explained calmly, "and the dogs were too excited when I returned."

The longer I sat with her, surrounded by the dogs, the more uncomfortable I became. Part of me was full of admiration at what she was able to do, but another part of me felt she had crossed a line—a boundary between what is rational and what is not—from which she could never return. My own three dogs were waiting for me at home, and to me, that felt like quite enough; three more than I ever imagined having, but now they were my own.

"Have you always been this way?" I asked, wondering if this might be something new—if perhaps she had come to "the dog thing" late, as I had.

"Always. Even when I was a little girl. My family has never understood it."

Patricia offered me a ride back to Ciudad Colón. She had to take one of the dogs to the vet, but this meant that first, she had to catch her. One might think this would have been easy with all of the surrounding chaos. How could any of the dogs have sensed the office-visit vibe that we were emitting? Yet the dog in question disappeared immediately, racing up to the top of the property and refusing to return. Patricia's assistant climbed on top of a horse and rode up to follow the dog, and this activity stirred up the entire property. As he continued to track the animal, the rest of the dogs began barking and chasing the horse as Patricia called out the poor dog's name—one that I now cannot remember. Finally, the dog came down the mountain and we were on our way.

I thought of what Carla had said and wondered what was correct. We humans have a tendency to see things in black and white, as good or bad, right or wrong. But the real world is more complicated than that.

• • •

The first time I had stayed in Ciudad Colón, I was the only

guest of the colony for most of three months. Eventually I was joined by an Italian sculptor, a German couple working on an enormous park installation, and an artist from Argentina. This time around, everyone was from the States. We shared our work with each other, and in our free time, we walked down to the village. On the way back up the mountain, everyone knew to stop and catch their breath at the gate of the white horse, wondering aloud at whether the walk would be possible if the horse weren't there to visit. In the evening we would share meals and sit to watch Thalia do her rounds around the farm. One night Thalia even came into my room, climbed onto the bed, and snored there till morning. Like the majority of Costa Rica's dogs, I discovered that Thalia had an owner, a Canadian woman, who allowed her to run on her own all day. And another woman, an American, kept a close eye on her.

So much had changed during the six years I had been away, including the buses. The old, run-down American school buses had been replaced with mostly new, adult-sized coaches. There were several new restaurants in town, including an Italian place in a converted house at the foot of the mountain. No dogs allowed. As I stood in the village waiting for the bus one evening with my fellow "colonists," I spotted a woman sitting on the opposite corner, in front of the new aquarium shop, with several dogs in crates on display. The Asociación was having an adoption fair.

I crossed the street and bent down to greet an awkward,

brindle-striped puppy. He looked just like Brando had, six years earlier, when I spotted him in the BARC shelter in Brooklyn, in the weeks after having to leave Duque behind.

"I have one just like this," I told the woman.

And two days later, I was home.

Ken,

We have three dogs, outside, on six acres in St. Amant. I know your area well. I worked at Place St. Charles and walked through that area every week or so at lunch. We have been to Bacchanal. I was the Guinness guy.

Our first dog (Bear) is part chow. He was dingy, worn, and hungry. He walked past the front of the property some 300 feet away from ten kids playing on a trampoline some fifteen years ago. His eyes, even from that distance, said, "I'm home." He hasn't left the property since.

The second dog (Snoopy) is short-haired and medium-sized. He's the dog everyone loves. When he found me, he was bony and tired . . . probably a poor hunting dog that was left to fend for himself when the season ended.

Sam is part husky and medium-sized. Kristi and I were visiting a friend at a trailer park and heard this constant barking. While she was inside, I visited this dog. He was chained to a tree next to a bayou, so wound around it that he couldn't reach his food or water. I knocked on the trailer and was met by the "man." When I asked about whether they wanted the dog, he said, "No, the kids didn't take care of it." I took the dog and put him in our van. When Kristi came out, she said, "Go get that dog!" I told her he was already in the van, and let's go before they change their mind.

Sam hasn't stopped smiling since. He runs down the driveway with his mouth open when it rains. He had

heartworm and was seriously aggressive toward Snoopy.
Snoopy and Sam got fixed. On the day that my youngest of
four daughters said, "Dad, you have to let Sam out of the dog
cage someday," Sam and Snoopy got into a fight. They fell
into our pond and nearly drowned each other. They came out,
shook off, and have been friends ever since. Boys will be boys.

    My daughters say we have had a hundred dogs. They
come and visit and they go. I don't know one of them that I
owned. They visited. I hope I was good for them. And yes,
they sit next to me when I read in the backyard and show
true affection, but I sense that they are so much more aware of
everything than I will ever be.

    Tom and Kristi

the stranger
beside me

───────────

Brando grew up in Manhattan, so his tastes were always somewhat more cultured than a country dog's might be. Brando enjoyed occasional meals at Esperanto on Avenue C, where the manager would bring out a plate of chorizo when he saw us pass. Or we would go to Dogz on Park for an eight-dollar hot dog at lunch. Our morning routine was a walk along the East River to the seaport, where we would share an egg sandwich from one of the coffee trucks and then sit on the pier watching as everyone else scurried to work. He attended art openings and literary readings. He would occasionally insist on entering the offices of the local AIDS clinic to visit the staff, or he might plant himself in the middle of the large farmers' market at Union Square. He listened to the local Spanish-language radio stations during the day, and occasionally, while sitting in a screening room on the other side of town, I found myself thinking, *Brando would love this movie.*

The idea of nature was as foreign to Brando as the suggestion to me that he was merely an animal. He liked to sit with the mice that had been glue-trapped in the apartment. He liked to visit with the rabbits at the pet store up the street, who would press their noses between the bars of their cages as Brando sprawled in front of them, pressing his own nose back against theirs. Watching squirrels was a spectator sport for him. The squirrels would dance around the limbs of their trees, then race down to wave their tails in Brando's face. At that, Brando would grin deliriously, like a businessman getting a lap dance. The idea of any spontaneous, tangible interaction with these creatures never seemed to cross his mind.

Then we moved to Florida and Zephyr moved in. Zephyr was a country dog, in touch with her prey drive. Brando and I were transfixed by her hunting expeditions in our small backyard. One day I looked out and saw Brando staring into the corner of the yard, unable to move. I discovered Zephyr there, under the bamboo, with the tail of a squirrel hanging from her mouth. "Drop it," I commanded, and she did, revealing that everything but the tail was gone.

Another time, I watched from the kitchen window as she stalked a bird across the lawn. I watched because I was in awe of her determination and focus. She wasn't allowing the impossibility of the task to stop her from making an attempt. Step by step she made her way toward the bird, freezing on two paws for a moment between steps. I was waiting for the moment when the bird caught on and flew out of range. But when Zephyr's shadow crossed the bird, the bird flew up and directly into Zephyr's mouth.

I raced out the door, calling "Drop it!" And miraculously, she did. The bird was startled, possibly even injured. I waited with Zephyr as it struggled to regain its composure. Just as it fluttered its wings again, Brando ran out from the house to scoop the injured bird into his mouth and run rings around the yard, showing off his newfound expertise as a hunter. This made me truly hysterical. I chased Brando, commanding him to drop it again, but he turned to Zephyr, taunting her by chomping on the bird once or twice. Finally, he did drop it, but it was too late.

Brando, it turned out, was an animal after all.

A few years later we moved to Mississippi, now joined by Sula. The backyard was enormous and overgrown, and turned into a lake every time there was heavy rain. I could let Brando and Zephyr out into the yard in the evenings, while fence-jumping Sula and I had to stay in the living room, just inside the door. One evening, I heard something—a strange rhythm, maybe, or an extra set of paws against the ground. In the beam of my flashlight, I caught Zephyr standing face-to-face with an enormous raccoon. This standoff lasted a split second, as Brando leapt from the darkness, took the raccoon's neck in his mouth, and shook it until it was dead. I have a sense that the raccoon made a horrific noise in its final moments, but the truth is that the only thing I could hear were my own terrified screams.

I brought the dogs into the house and went back into the yard, armed with as many plastic garbage bags as I could find. I used the bags as gloves, wrapping the dead raccoon before bagging it. The package was enormous, and I was torn between sympathy for the animal inside, disgust, and fear. Fear, particularly, of rabies, although I knew that the chances of getting rabies from a dead raccoon were slim. Once I had wrapped the body several times, I lifted it into my arms. I planned to carry it to the front of my driveway, so that the next morning I could call the appropriate authorities to have it removed. But carrying the dead weight of a large raccoon was too much for me. This was the fall of 2004, and the electricity in my heart had stopped working, although I hadn't figured that out yet. Carrying anything heavier than a pound or two was more than I could handle. So I struggled to the fence and threw the bag over the side, assuming it could rest there until morning.

Inside the house, I found Brando curled up at the foot of my bed, waiting for my return. This was familiar. This was routine. But in bed with his weight leaning against my side, it was difficult to get the image out of my mind: the raccoon caught in his jaw, its neck snapping.

Brando leaned in for a kiss and I turned my head away.

• • •

Months later, on an uncharacteristically cold March night, Zephyr ran in from the yard with a look of alarm on her face. I followed her out and found Brando standing over the still body of an adult possum. It took a moment longer for my eyes to adjust to the moonlight and see what had the dogs transfixed: tiny, thumb-sized baby possums wriggling through the dirt, trying to find warmth.

I'll never know what actually happened that night, but I felt certain that Brando had once again been the killer, and that Zephyr—being a woman, after all—saw the babies and felt something had to be done. (This is, I realize, somewhat insane and illogical—beginning with my claim that Zephyr is a *woman*.) I took the dogs back inside where Sula was already settled in and returned to the yard with a flashlight, only to discover that while the babies were still crawling through the cold earth, the mother had disappeared.

Of course, that's why they call it "playing possum."

I searched the yard and found the mother's body again, a few yards away, in an overgrown cluster of grass and weeds. I returned to the house and waited to see if she would move on her own, but when I checked again, she still lay where I had left her.

I went to the kitchen and found a soup spoon and a large cardboard box. Outside again, I lifted the babies, one by one, into the box. Baby possums are marsupial; these little guys were all small enough to fit comfortably in the spoon. They were pale and hairless, almost transparent. My heart—which by now had been fixed with a pacemaker—was pounding with fear. What would happen if I touched one of them? I didn't want to poison them with my scent. I was hoping there was still a chance that the mother could be revived.

Back in the kitchen, I rinsed out a plastic quart container of milk and filled it with warm water. Once it was settled in the box, the babies found their way to it and gathered around.

I moved them into the spare room and shut the door, then returned to my bed, where the three dogs were waiting for me. This was our custom on cold nights: all of the dogs burrowing into me from each side, trying to keep warm. Now I had another, more important obligation: to slip from beneath my warm blanket of dogs and check on the possum babies in the next room. Throughout the night, I lifted the milk bottle from their box and refilled it with warm tap water before replacing it and returning to my bed to pretend to sleep. Brando lifted his head with curiosity and moved into the warm spot I was vacating, so when I returned, I had to slip myself back between the sleeping dogs' bodies, just as I had slipped the warm milk container between the little possums, whose mother Brando had killed.

When you rescue a dog—or a cat—other people are included in the narrative that runs through your head, powering your actions. If you are honest with yourself, you realize that you don't think only of the animal. You think, too, of the lucky person who will end up living with this dog, and how both of their lives will be changed once they come together.

I could not find an equivalent narrative for rescuing baby possums. They were not going to grow into companion animals. They would become large rodents who would, if they were lucky, invade other people's yards, looking for whatever it is possums look for out there. I wasn't doing anyone any favors. I didn't know where I could take them or who would be interested in doing the real work of saving them.

And I couldn't fathom leaving them to die on their own.

Miraculously, they survived their first night outside the warmth of their mother's body. In the morning, I called around looking for a place to turn them in. There was a vet on the opposite side of town, someone said. They had a grant for such things. I carried the box into the waiting room and explained why I was there. The receptionist nodded and took the box from my hands. I returned to my empty car, wondering what would become of them.

At home, the dogs were waiting inside, waiting to finally be let back into the yard. The mother's body was still there, with the lifeless body of one of her young clinging to the fur of her stomach. I spoke on the phone with a woman at Animal Control, trying to decide if it was their call, or whether it was now a matter for the sanitation department instead. Eventually a man came out driving a white truck. I let him in through the gate and he lifted the possum by the tail, carried her to the truck, and tossed her into the back.

I let the dogs roam free again to explore the yard. They checked out the spot where the night before there had been babies crawling on the ground, and when they found nothing there, they returned to their usual routine.

Inside, at my desk, I sat typing with Sula, my pit bull, sitting on my lap. She was completely unaware of the drama that had unfolded around her the previous night. But she knew, and reminded me, of how lucky we both were to be alive and to be home.

Hi Ken,

My brother is currently living in Los Angeles, and his birthday present to me on December 28 was The Dogs Who Found Me. *I started reading it last night and I can't put it down! (I don't want the book to end.) I understand why he bought me the book, as I do the same things as you! It first started in 1991 when I "found" my beloved late Susie. I was heavily pregnant at the time, and I found her shaking and distraught; the pads on her feet were raw, and she only had one eye. I found her in exactly the same place where I had been involved in a car crash six years previous; my best friend had died that day, aged sixteen years, and I had smashed my femur. You can imagine the connection I had with Susie. I learned that she had been running around desperate for hours, and nobody had stopped for her. Why? Well, I'm glad they didn't, as I like to think she was destined for me. From 1991 to 2005, I "rescued" when I could, dogs here and dogs there. I used to wish I could drive around blindfolded, as I ran out of potential homes!*

Then in 2005 it all changed with Sky and her pups. To cut a long story short, it came about that I made contact with "Christine" (perhaps your Pam), and the fostering and rescuing snowballed. All lovely dogs with their own stories/baggage, even though most often I am just guessing their stories.

As I type this, fireworks are starting to go off in the neighborhood in preparation for the New Year. My own four dogs are chilled and don't care about the noise, but I can see that our current foster, Sam, is not very happy at all!

I will close here before I ramble on and on and tell you all about my Casey, Daisy, Sally, and Sky. But I just wanted you to know how wonderful it is to read your book. I have never e-mailed an author before, or ever had the inclination to!

Take care. I will enjoy reading the rest of your book, and all the best to you, Brando, Zephyr, and Sula in 2007!

With love from Emma
(Keighley, West Yorkshire, England)

sula's
bad mood
and her bad tummy
and her bad platelets
and her bad vet

THE DAY WE MOVED FROM MISSISSIPPI TO NEW ORLEANS, I got a call from the vet to let me know that the cyst removed from Sula's chest wasn't cancerous after all. I had prepared myself for the worst, if that's possible, but once again the worst didn't come. The cyst—pink, hairless, alarmingly large—had appeared seemingly overnight.

This was the summer of 2005 and Sula was getting leery of the vet. A year earlier, after having surgery on her face and heartworm treatment, she still thought of vets as the greatest thing on earth, but her attitude toward them began to change around the time I was hospitalized. Maybe she was inspired by the anxiety caused by my own illness. Maybe she became spoiled by the hours I eventually spent at home. Or maybe it was a bad vet experience, something I didn't know about, that led to her aversion.

In the fall of 2004, she had suffered through a long digestive disaster that required—for no good reason—multiple consultations, tests, and fees. It was ultimately diagnosed as giardia, but even after treatment, her stomach was never the same. She had been vomiting and having tarry diarrhea, all of which was accompanied by her suddenly becoming aggressive around food. Food aggression isn't all that uncommon among a pack of dogs, but since she had never exhibited this behavior previously, I was worried that she now felt the need to growl over her food before eating it.

At the time we were living in Mississippi, and I took her to the most expensive vet in town, where she somehow rarely managed to see an actual doctor. Instead we would talk to vet techs who would consult with an unseen doctor in the next room. That should have been a sign. Eventually, after weeks of visits and tests and consultations, they ran a test for giardia, something they had discouraged me from doing earlier because of the expense. When it came back positive, Sula was treated with Flagyl and Panacur, and I wondered why we had waited for the test results to come back at all, before starting with these common medications.

Once she had been treated, her charming personality came back again—for a while. But that winter, after I'd unexpectedly been hospitalized, Sula began exhibiting unusual behavior again. She growled at me when I put on my shoes.

She didn't want me leaving the house. She pushed her food out of her dish and then guarded it as stubbornly as she refused to eat it.

Once, when I absentmindedly left a box of biscuits on the floor, she and Zephyr got into a fight. Later, when we had all calmed down a bit, I notice Sula had been bleeding. There was blood in her crate, on her paws . . . but no wound. The most I could find was a small abrasion on the scruff of her neck, like a paper cut, and I wondered if, as with a paper cut, the blood was worse than the actual wound.

I contacted a few friends, all of whom suggested that Sula might need to be put down. I asked my friend Julia Lane in New Orleans if she had any other ideas. "Have you tested her for thyroid?" she asked. Julia had recently had a problem with one of her rescues, and discovered that a thyroid problem was to blame. Once the animal's thyroid levels were balanced, the aggressive behavior went away.

I got online—always a mistake when researching a homemade diagnosis—and typed in my terms. *Thyroid aggression* brought up thousands of references for problems that were seen in dogs, along with various therapies one could use. I typed in *thyroid pit bull* and found thousands of references to pit bulls suffering from thyroid problems. (It should be noted that thyroid problems can be found in all kinds of dogs, particularly purebred.) I typed in *thyroid pit bull aggression* and nothing came up that put the three things together. I wondered how many pit bulls might have undiagnosed thyroid problems, since the most visible symptom—aggression—might be something people took for granted in the breed.

Our expensive vet was reluctant to run the tests when I told her what the symptoms were.

"It's because she's a pit bull," she said when I described Sula's growling at the other dogs and snarling around their food.

"But she's never acted that way before," I said.

"She just grew into it," she said. "I have a pit bull, and I love her, but she doesn't like other dogs."

"But this seems different," I said. It didn't seem to matter that I was willing to pay for the expensive thyroid test. A few days later, I left Sula at the vet for the weekend while a dogsitter watched Brando and Zephyr. I was driving Theo, the rottweiler, to his new home in Florida. As I left the waiting area, Sula tried to chase after me, and when she reached the end of her leash, she turned and lunged at the vet tech who was holding the other end. I grabbed the leash and led Sula into the back myself. I began to understand where at least some of her anxiety was coming from. The barking was frantic, and many of the cages were covered with blankets, so you could hear the dogs, but not see them or what they were about to do. Sula clearly didn't want to be there. As I led her into the empty bin, two dogs tried to squeeze out of the space above hers, snapping viciously in our direction.

"Can you run those tests while she is here?" I asked. And before picking her up a few days later, I called to check again.

"Oh, yes," I was told. "We pulled the blood to send."

"But did you pull enough blood?" I asked. "I don't want to have to bring her back again."

"Yes," they said. And yes again, when I asked in the waiting area, and Sula stood with her front paws wrapped around my waist and her head pressed into my stomach.

"So we won't have to come back and take more blood?" I asked.

"No, we have plenty."

• • •

Of course, three days later I got a call telling me that they didn't have enough blood. We would have to return and start over again. By this time Brando had started seeing a new vet, in Petal, a small town just east of where we lived. Brando has never been a fan of going to the doctor. In Florida, I had to carry him from the car to the office when it was time for his annual shots. After Sula's experiences with the bad vet, I knew that we needed to look elsewhere for him. Brando had never been to a female vet before, and this office was staffed entirely with women. All of his anxiety associations began to dim. I drove over with Sula and asked them to do the test.

"We can do a preliminary test while you wait," they said. "If nothing shows up, there's no point in doing the whole thing."

This wasn't the information that Julia had given me, but I agreed all the same. They took her sample into another room and returned a few minutes later to tell me everything was normal. I was stunned. I had been hoping to find the source of her unhappiness, and to solve it.

"Well, actually, her platelet count is abnormally low, but it's so low that it must be a mistake. We can run the test again, and I'll call you."

Sula and I headed out to the car, but we hadn't even reached the parking lot exit when the vet came running out to us.

"There is something wrong," she said. "I need you to come in."

Once we'd returned to the office, the vet said, "I think it's ehrlichiosis." And I said, "What?" I learned that it's a tick-borne illness with autoimmune effects, including lameness, kidney disease, and anemia, which can sometimes be mistaken for leukemia. Another version, babesia, is particularly common in pit bulls. The prescription was a long course of antibiotics.

"There's another expensive test we can run," the vet suggested, "but I think we can just run a test again in a few weeks and see if this does the trick."

And it did. Sula returned to normal, and a few weeks later I got a call from our previous incompetent vet, asking why we hadn't returned for them to fill more vials with Sula's blood.

"We've taken care of it," I said.

Apparently this was not the correct response. The test was already paid for, they said, so it should be run. I asked them why they had charged my credit card if they hadn't had enough blood for the test to be run in the first place.

"We didn't know that there wasn't enough blood until we had already ordered the test."

"That doesn't make sense," I said. "I want a refund."

"We can't refund the money. The lab charged us already. They had to try to run the test before they could tell us they needed more blood. Maybe we can give you a discount on the second run."

"No," I said. "There isn't going to be a second run. She's already been treated. Can I speak with the doctor?"

"I've already spoken with the doctor," the voice on the other end said.

And so on, until I realized that I just needed to move on.

• • •

Like bad vets, giardia can be tough to escape. Once Sula had regained her health, she decided she liked not ever having to leave home. She liked watching television. She liked taking walks to visit and kiss the seemingly abandoned children at a house down the street. She liked lying face-to-face with Zephyr on my bed and playing a variation of thumb wrestling, in which they substituted their heads for thumbs. But any variation of this routine produced intestinal problems, and these disruptions were sometimes followed by crabbiness.

All of this was understandable. I get crabby, too, when my stomach is in distress. In college, I had digestive problems for years and assumed that it was normal, or caused by the dorm food, or any number of other things, before settling on the reality that it was anxiety. In high school, my mother took a caseful of Tagamet along on a three-month tour of Europe. Apparently weak stomachs run in the Foster family, including the foster dogs.

But I'm a hypochondriac on behalf of my dogs, so I continued searching websites for solutions. I'm not sure I'd recommend this as a solution for anyone else. Inevitably, whatever terms you type in, you end up with predicted fatalities. Everything is associated with cancer, or worse. In Sula's case I discovered that giardia might not ever be completely cured. It simply goes dormant, or "encapsulates" in the intestine, and can be unleashed by the rise in stomach acid that accumulates with stress.

What's more alarming is that if I hadn't obsessively Googled on her behalf and insisted on tests that nobody wanted to run, Sula might not be with us today. Not just because of her tummy problem, but also because of her blood, and because of the assumptions people make, including some vets, based on the way she looks.

When the cyst appeared as a blemish beneath the white fur of Sula's chest, I noticed it, but told myself it wasn't a big thing. A few weeks later, it had become, quite literally, a big thing. I had seen these things before, usually around the mouth or chin of a dog, usually much smaller than what this had become. It was the size of a dime, then a quarter, but irregular in its shape.

"It's probably nothing," the vet agreed, but a needle biopsy came back with irregular cells. "We'll have to remove it, and send it to the lab."

I walked Sula back to the kennels. There was a blanket covering the kennel doors, and the dogs behind it were barking at the pace of machine-gun fire. Sula panicked and tried to run. The staff directed me into the surgery room. Sula was trying to jump into my arms. There's nothing more horrifying than seeing a happy dog overcome with panic like this. While I held her, they approached with the injection.

"This is going to be disturbing for you," they said. "It's going to be like she's died."

Sula looked into my eyes and then went blank, then limp in my arms. When I returned a few hours later, the cyst had been removed and packed to send to a lab and Sula was doing her happy dance in her kennel.

"I thought she might be groggy when I arrived," I said. The staff laughed at me and said, "Not this dog."

• • •

While we were packing to move to New Orleans, I kept thinking about the tests, and when the results would arrive. Would I go through with the move if I knew Sula was going to die? This is how my melodramatic mind works. If the worst happened, what would we do to survive?

At the end of July, I packed up the car, headed down the highway to New Orleans, and within a few miles it was the car, not Sula, that died. I rented another car. While I was transferring my stuff from the dead car to the live one, Sula was determined not to be left behind. She jumped against the hatchback door and balanced on the bumper. It was clear she wanted to be the first inside.

I checked my messages as we left town again, and heard "The tests are back. Everything is fine." Two hours later we were entering our new home in New Orleans.

Four weeks later, Hurricane Katrina arrived.

Dear Ken,

My dog Henry and I met you at the SPCA event in Audubon Park a few weeks ago, and I bought a copy of your book, which you autographed for my husband. I just finished reading it, and I wanted to tell you how much I enjoyed it.

You probably don't recall this, but Henry (my part schnauzer pup) was living under our Uptown home when we returned from our evacuation after the storm. After a few weeks of feeding him filet and pork tenderloin (he didn't like dog food at the time because he had been living on garbage for weeks), he finally decided one day to come into our home and allowed us to be his parents. It has been six months since Henry landed in our lives, and I cannot imagine what our lives were like before him.

Your book truly captures what life with a dog is like, and it was a pleasure to read. Thank you for sharing your stories with me and the rest of the world.

Fellow dog lover,
Mary Margaret

dogs on desire street:
a dog's-eye view of the recovery

IT'S EARLY OCTOBER OF 2005, AND A DAY AFTER RETURNING to our mostly abandoned New Orleans neighborhood, Zephyr and I decide to go to the park. Before the storm, I walked my dogs together, but with strays roaming the area in packs, I'm now taking them out one at a time. Zephyr's looking for birds—there are none. I'm looking for people—not many of them, either. But at least we're home.

In the distance I see a dog rooting through a pile of debris. It's Rosalind, a dog I met before the storm. A few days before the evacuation, I found her wandering the streets and took her to the park. "Have they let her out again?" one of our pre-Katrina neighbors said. Her owners were out of town. Her dogsitters were not paying attention. When I spot her post-K, I assume she's been on the streets the entire time. She won't let me come near her.

Later in the day, I walk two blocks to Markey's Bar, where everyone is drinking and exchanging stories of what happened to them, before, during, after. There is graffiti all over along the way, pleas for help painted in large letters on the streets. Stolen buses scattered around. Rosalind is sitting out in front of the bar, waiting for a handout. I take the seat next to her and check her collar. There's a number; I call.

We're safe in Texas, the message says, *but we'd rather be in New Orleans. Beep.*

"I'm glad you're safe in Texas," I say. "I'm in New Orleans, sitting on the street with your dog." I leave my number. Rosalind follows me almost the whole way home, then turns and runs away as we approach the door. Inside, I pile the dogs into my bed. We sleep in a giant ball. I wake up in the middle of the night and find half of Sula's leash next to me.

"You didn't eat this did you?" I ask. She doesn't answer, which means that she did.

In the morning, Zephyr and I return to the park. She's waiting for birds. I'm waiting for people. The gate opens at the far end of the park. It's Rosalind, walking with her owner.

"I left a message for you last night," I say, trying to figure it out. Then the simple solution hits me: She hasn't changed her message since she returned from Texas.

"Oh," the owner says. "She just wandered off the porch for a minute."

"She was sitting in front of Markey's," I say.

Ms. Owner turns and looks at Roz. She looks back at me. "Really?" she asks. She is clearly embarrassed.

"Maybe she picked it up from watching all the strays," I suggest. "She was very convincing."

• • •

In the middle of the night, Sula begins coughing up the leash. I sit with her and cut small pieces loose as it hangs out her mouth, then wait for her to cough up a little more. There is no emergency vet. There is no vet. And, a few days later, when I nearly poke my eye out on a branch that is lower than it was before the storm, I realize that there isn't much human care available, either. There's no good reason for any of us to be here besides the fact that it's home.

Brando and Zephyr watch me chop the leash piece by piece from Sula's mouth. They find the whole thing mesmerizing and horrible.

In the morning, Brando finds a new friend: Dixie, the Catahoula/pit bull who is displaced, along with her owner, from the French Quarter. Zephyr pairs up with Maddie, another little mix of some kind. Maddie's owner is Dar, who lost a house in Mid-City. Zephyr and Maddie chase each other while Dar and I talk about the city, or about Maddie and Zephyr on days when the subject of the city is too grim. Sula has a brief flirtation with Oliver, who lives in the recording studio across from the park. *Good choice*, I think, as if I want her to marry well. But the romance is short-lived.

One day, alone in the park, I hear a car slow down, and someone says, "Look at that dog." I step from behind a tree to see who it is. A black van pulls out, speeding the wrong way up the street. On the side someone has painted KATRINA ANIMAL RESCUE. A few nights earlier, a police officer returned home to find his rottweiler had been "rescued." Brando and Sula are back at the house, alone, up the street. Zephyr and I take off running to find them, safe, of course, but happy to see us again.

• • •

We live on Piety Street, which is just a block from Desire—and no, the two do not ever intersect. That's always the first question. There used to be a Desire bus that ran slowly through the neighborhood, coughing up exhaust along the way, but as far as I can tell, that bus has been replaced by one that simply says BYWATER or BYWATER-MARIGNY, and these days, chances of seeing that are slim. After the storm and the evacuation, we returned to find many of these buses scattered around the neighborhood. On St. Claude Avenue, one bus was parked haphazardly across the neutral ground, its route sign frozen on this incomplete message: PLEASE CALL.

Here in the proximity of Tennessee Williams's characters, Brando's name takes on a new layer of associations. Someone in the shelter where I found him gave him the name, and I didn't see any point in changing it. No matter how much it initially embarrassed me.

"I didn't pick the name," I would announce as soon as anyone asked the question. Eventually, I forgot there was any other Brando aside from mine. When Marlon Brando died, I remember someone in the park saying, "You must be sad."

"Why?" I asked, completely disconnected from any association with the dead Brando.

In fact, at the dog park across from the Piety Street recording studio, there are at least three Brandos. In addition to my enormous brindle Brando, there is a Jack Russell and a rottie. Randi, the Jack Russell's owner, frequently claims that hers is the original Brando. "To this dog park," she adds. The rottie is new, adopted to keep a Stella husky company. "She should pick a different name," Randi says. "She should choose Mitch or Tennessee." I imagine a dog with Karl Malden's nose.

"Or even just Stanley," I suggest.

There are actually more Stella dogs than Brandos: a Great Dane, the husky, and several dainty mutts. Throughout the day, it is possible to see one human or another standing at the gate to the park, yelling "Stella! Stella!"

• • •

In line for unemployment, the woman ahead of me is talking about her dog.

"We had to leave him behind," she says. "He's a pit bull. We didn't have a car. Our neighbors gave us a ride out, but there wasn't room for him. We thought the storm wasn't

coming, and we'd be back in the morning. We got six feet of
water." She keeps going, even though I'm not sure I want to
hear. "We got a call two weeks later, someone telling us the
condition of the house. 'I could hear your dog in the yard,' he
says, and we think that can't be. But we had to be sure, so we
drove eight hours back, and there he is."

"Where is he now?" I ask.

"In Texas," she says. "He's not leaving my son's side."

Behind me, a man is talking about his dogs. A rescue
group has them, but they want to neuter them before they return them. "That's the only reason I have them," he says. "If
they're going to cut them, I don't want them to return." When
a woman asks him why he hasn't filled out his entire form, he
says without hesitation, "Because I don't know how to read."
Yet the man is sharp; I listen to him on his cell phone, calling
his network of friends telling them what to expect.

• • •

Scott pulls up in his red hatchback and unpacks his greyhounds like a set of fancy luggage. They scatter across the
park, posing, frozen in a tableau. Macy was kicked off the
track the day before her second birthday. Shasta was given
up by her breeder when she was five years old. Rhubarb, the
male of the trio, is beige, or "red"—hence the name, although rhubarb doesn't grow in Louisiana. Still, it's better
than Don L's Sydney G, which is what he was called back
on the track.

As months pass, more dogs arrive. Molly, a black Lab mix, moves in from Gentilly. Her folks eventually add Jax, another black Lab, to the mix.

Others are old-timers, from before the storm. Max and Heidi arrive each morning chauffeured in their contractor's trucks. Aries, another Doberman, comes over from Congress Street driven by Valerie, with her NOTCHOC personalized plate. Rascal walks with Mark Gonzalez, dispensing treats. Cole barks at the fence while his owner tries to talk off her hangover. Flash, the resident basset hound, flops his ears back and forth while Russell tells the story again about the National Guard arriving at their door.

Gil and his owner give up and return to New York. Cole's owner moves on without him, and when he arrives with new people, he's so content it's hard to recognize him.

Brando and I keep waiting for the return of Grong Grong, his little double from before the storm. Finally, after our book comes out, I hear from a reporter in Memphis. "Grong Grong is my cousin," she says. "He and his family are living up here."

• • •

Shawn has a picture of Oliver on the day he was found, just after Hurricane Cindy, a storm most of us subsequently forgot. Taken on July 28, 2005, there is Oliver, palm-sized, hiding between a brick wall and a potted plant. He looks too serious to be a puppy, and the look remains today: stoic, skeptical, except when it's time to play. Shawn and Mark are living in the recording studio now, waiting for their house to be repaired.

Sula might be over her fling with Oliver, but she keeps her eye out for any famous musicians who may be there. Why bother with a dog when there's a chance of getting serenaded by Elvis Costello (who, it turns out, is only good for a polite wave of his hand)? One afternoon Ted Leo is unpacking some instruments for a session that's about to begin. It isn't until he says, "Hello, crazy doggie," that I recognize him. He and Sula embrace as he continues talking to her like somewhat of a madman. I stand on the sidelines and never once think to mention that I have tickets for his show that evening. Not to him. Certainly not to Sula.

This obsession with musicians recalls Brando's celebrity-obsessed puppyhood in the East Village, where he got attention from Sandra Bullock (who tried to hide behind a bush while watching him drink from a hose), John Leguizamo (who lived a few buildings away), and Edie Falco. Edie walked her dog Marley over from the West Side early each morning, and Brando would position himself in front of her bench, staring with his mouth agape. "I'm sorry about that," I would say each time. And Edie would answer, "For what?"

• • •

At the voodoo shop across the street from our house, a female husky stands guard. The shop is open, and she is the shop dog. Inside, you can pay for a consultation, or buy a chicken foot to hang above the door. You have to hope that your dog doesn't notice the chicken foot, otherwise your good luck streak might be gone. Brando does not approve of huskies, particularly just outside our door. He does not approve of Maddie and Sophie, who come over from Desire Street, dragging Elizabeth along. He prefers the Doberman, Jinx, and his co-dog, Bella, and Sean and Janet, the humans who are attached to them at the leash. Janet and Sean have moved here from Lakeview, and over the course of a year, they move from the house on Dauphine to another one further down the street on Gallier. They are trying to decide what to do with their Lakeview house.

Brando keeps checking the Dauphine address, even after he's figured out where they've moved. One day, a car pulls up as Brando sniffs the stoop, and a whole new family pops out of the car to greet him. This is unusual: People who don't know Brando generally aren't interested in running up to him—he's too big, and his stripes are too strange.

"We used to have a dog just like this," they say.

I'm looking for a new house, too. I check out a place at the end of the neighborhood. The house next door still has graffiti from the storm: TWO DOGS. It doesn't say whether they were dead or alive, rescued or left behind, but one thing is certain—they haven't returned. I remember parking in front of this house the day before the evacuation; I remember two pit bulls greeting me on my way home.

On a weekend when Janet and Sean are out of town, I end up keeping an eye on Jinx and Bella and their two foster

Dobermans, Lyric and Colt. A thunderstorm rolls in. I spend two days running between our houses, trying to get timid dogs to step outside again in the rain. Sula's not having it. Lyric and Colt try to run under their house. When the storm finally clears, I turn up in the park with what seems like the wrong group of dogs. "I'm dogsitting," I explain.

• • •

There are two dogs in the park. One is Zephyr. The other appears to be her twin. They begin chasing each other, diving beneath each other's feet. We watch in fascination, as if we have never seen this behavior before.

I think about Hurricane Agnes, when the floods improbably reached Central Pennsylvania, and, without electricity for five days, neighbors gathered at our house to watch two kittens play for hours, as if it was something on TV.

Or how in NYC after 9/11, the dog park was full of people and dogs chasing each other, just like it had been the day before, even though everything had been transformed. The routine of our dogs was something we could be certain of.

Suddenly I'm on the ground, and the dogs are on top of me. Zephyr's licking my face, followed by her new friend. I'm laughing. The man with the dog bends over and introduces himself. And introduces his dog, who is still kissing me.

Her name is Lolita Bradbury.

• • •

On the neighborhood's online forum, people are talking about the people in the park. *Be careful of them*, one says. *Don't believe anything they say.*

In New York, people used to gather around the dog run as if they were at a zoo. Who were they studying—the dogs, or their owners? One day I was watching, too, along with two young women who had their eye on a Jack Russell terrier who was racing around in the snow wearing a T-shirt. The dog's owner removed the shirt and he continued running. One of the women turned to the other and said, with an inappropriate degree of awe, "Now he's completely naked." That's when I decided to get a dog of my own, so I could stand on the opposite side of the fence from them.

There are phases to recovery. There are phases to grief. There is a time when everyone is unified in their efforts, in their anger, and then most people turn inward again, get suspicious and distant.

Whatever they are talking about, I wouldn't believe it, someone types on the forum.

Maybe they think of us the way the Puritans thought of the witches. Maybe our dogs are our familiars. They give us a power that puts others on edge.

• • •

Uptown, at Belladonna Day Spa, Kim Dudek is sponsoring free microchipping for a weekend at the start of hurricane season. Tents are set up and people and dogs are lined up for blocks around the site of her newest venture, Belladoggie. Somehow no one expected this, but the turnout suggests something about the way our minds are working, as the anniversary approaches. People are standing for hours with their dogs, in the rain. I'm supposed to be signing books, but I spend most of my time answering questions about microchips and how they work. I watch the crowd, from Uptown, Mid-City, the Westbank, Bywater, Treme, Marigny. Pit bulls, teacup dogs, mutts, recent rescues.

Kim wrote to me after reading the book:

I am you in female form. And ever since reading your book, they are finding me faster than I can find good homes for them. So I now have six dogs at home!! Six is just too many, but we are handling it.

I wrote to Pam at Ruff Rescue about one of my Katrina fosters that I have had since January, and she graciously placed him on her website. His name is Sarge, and he is a brindled Mastiff/Lab mix. I found him while feeding [stray dogs] in Lakeview, and we finally got him off the streets on December 31. He weighed fifty pounds—rather slender for a mastiff. He was heartworm-positive and not fixed. He did not sleep for three days. He sat bolt upright and patrolled.

On the fourth day, he jumped in my bed and collapsed into my arms and slept. It took him a long time to learn what a treat was, what a plate of food was for, what a toy did, and why I wiped his eye sand from his eyes all day long. He has crooked teeth and needs braces. He has finally grown incredibly fond of my four shar-pei, who have taught him to be with other dogs. They taught him to share, when enough is enough, how to eat a treat without losing it to one of the other dogs, and how to kiss.

Sarge was obviously well trained by someone who also trained him to be VERY protective—too protective for my taste. I have worked with him to try and get him to be OK with people being on the "other" side of the fence. He sounds like a lunatic for the fifteen minutes he feels he has to carry on. I wrote Pam and asked for her assistance in finding a great home for him. So, thank you for sharing her information.

Oddly enough, I was looking through the Urban Dog issue in which you were featured and saw that fabulous picture of you and your gorgeous big dog on your lap. Sarge could be your dog's twin. I was so surprised.

But Sarge has proven to be hard to place. Now and then I stop into Kim's office at the back of the spa, and we exchange the latest. She's fitting a house with kennels outside of town to be ready for the next evacuation. She's hired a trainer for Sarge, still trying to find him a home. She's learning how to do acupuncture for dogs, and tells me how the procedure has cured one of her fosters, Dag, a lame pit bull. She sends photos of him laying on a blanket on the floor as a team of women work him over with their massage techniques. I wonder if it might help Brando, who is showing signs of his own hip problems.

Eventually Sarge does find a home with his trainer. And Kim takes the energy she once devoted to him and gives it to the next dog down the line.

• • •

Jane's dog, a large, shepherdy thing, lost a leg to cancer. She comes to the park and rolls around on her back, waving her three legs for everyone to see. Monique, from around the corner, brings Singer, her blue-eyed Catahoula. Jack, a diabetic golden retriever, wrestles with Oliver, and with little Brando, and with anyone who climbs on his back.

Thelonious comes over from Louisa Street. He lives with Julie, in the house behind ours. "I'm having the fence repaired," Julie tells me. "So if you suddenly see an Airedale wandering in your yard . . ." While Julie talks, Thelonious does his daily humping.

Snowy, heir to Markey's bar, goes from person to person, soliciting pets while simultaneously hoisting her nose in the air. Oliver, still living directly across the street, has become accustomed to having the park at his disposal. Shawn and Mark let him run for hours, while keeping an eye on him from their open door. But lately Oliver hasn't been feeling very playful. He runs out the park door and refuses to return.

"Just knock on the studio door," someone suggests.

Oliver wants to be with Shawn now. He doesn't want her out of his sight. Shawn has been diagnosed with cancer, and her treatments have somehow managed to fall in line with the holidays: Thanksgiving, New Year's, Mardi Gras, etc.

"He's become such a mama's boy," Shawn says. I tell her how Zephyr put her ear to my chest after my pacemaker was installed. How Brando responded when two weeks later my leg was ripped open on a post office door. I returned with stitches and a bandage up the side of my leg, and he had a seizure, something that had only happened once before: when Howard Dean withdrew from the presidential race.

"They understand everything," I tell her. "He knows what's going on."

Oliver stands sideways in front of her, marking his turf, protecting her from the world. Shawn looks down at Oliver and says, in exactly the same tone of voice she'd use for a person, "I don't know how I'd get through this without you."

• • •

Molly and Jax are moving to Boston; they're bringing their owners along. Gil is back for a visit, but it's obvious he's got New York on his mind, and in a few weeks he and Pat head back north. We make fun of the idea of them in the cold. In their absence we'll make room for new dogs, new people. There will be more Stellas, more Brandos. Yet never a dog named Blanche, after the one character who depended on strangers—and then went mad. Elizabeth arrives from her house on Desire Street and lets her two dogs roam while she runs the perimeter of the park with headphones on. She's having to multitask, we think, now that she's in love.

Our dogs see us through more than they put us through.

Hello, Ken.

My name is Jessica, and I just wanted to drop a line. I recently picked up your book, in New Orleans of all places. (I currently live outside Washington, D.C.) I'm a freelance travel writer and was in New Orleans to write, pump money into the economy, and to let my puppy pee in Cafe Du Monde. (The latter was not planned.)

First, a little about my freelancing. I've been driving around the country since last June (and five months in 2005), writing about the randomness I get into. I just came home a few weeks ago. I saw lots of stray dogs in my eleven months of traveling. It was heartbreaking, especially the nursing mothers begging for food. I almost took a few of these, but didn't want to separate a mother from a litter of nursing pups. Also, I suffered from the same type of problem you and Brando had in your early days of rescuing—no space! A studio apartment is bad, but a large-breed dog living long-term in a packed Honda Civic is damn near impossible. So I took to leaving takeout containers of food and water around wherever I saw one . . . which was usually on Indian reservations.

But this brings me to my next point, and a good one—my Darby. (I'm tearing up as I'm writing this . . . I know you know how it is.) I was in Kayenta, Arizona, on the Navajo reservation, the week before Halloween. I didn't need gas, but I needed a bathroom. And there she was, a tiny black-and-white border collie puppy, all of six pounds, barely eight weeks old, stomach distended, scared of people, starving, with lice, and limping heavily.

"Whose dog is this?" I asked the attendant, who ignored me. "Whose is it?" I demanded.

"Somebody threw it."

"What?"

He stared off into space, speaking softly. "Somebody threw it out of a truck."

BASTARDS!!!

"Is anyone helping it?" He just shrugged.

So when I came out of the bathroom I bought a bag of Purina and a newspaper for the seat, and Darby—named after an old blind hobo companion in a Tom Waits song— and I set off for Durango, Colorado, the nearest big town, which was sure to have a shelter. (Sadly, there are no shelters on reservations, the places that need them most.) I called en route, but was told that because Darby was from Arizona, they could not take her, because their jurisdiction ended at the county line. I tried anyway, but they saw my Maryland license plates and knew it was me. The local no-kill was full. Where did that leave us? Here I was with a puppy, who had what turned out to be a broken hip and a broken leg, no place to stay, and barely any money.

But Durango came out of the woodwork to help us! Mr. Foster, you would have been so amazed to see it! No one *wanted to take on a puppy with that many vet bills right off the bat, but the town came together and raised over $2,000 in just one weekend so I could pay for her surgery! We were taken in by a nice girl for two weeks while Darby was evaluated, fixed, and recovering. Everywhere I went, people said, "Oh, you're the Dog Girl!" Darby was the toast of the town. I still get misty thinking about how wonderful people were to us. And they all said, "You didn't find her. She found you."*

To which I could only say, "And I'm so lucky."

So weeks later, while Darby and I were in New Orleans (and she was still wearing her cone), I saw your book on display at the used bookstore in the French Quarter and I had to pick it up. I loved having her with me in the city. I'm familiar with New Orleans, but this time I was able to see it through Darby's eyes. (And the waiters at Cafe Du Monde fell in love with her as we were waiting for our carry-out beignets, and insisted that the two of us come inside and sit down, which is how she ended up not only christening the tile, but also grabbing a beignet off someone else's table and wrestling with it, making powdered sugar fly everywhere! I was mortified, but people were laughing. How can you be mad at a puppy?)

Please take good care of yourself and your dog(s), and maybe someday we could get our "children" together for a playdate.

All the best,
Jessica

a unique
dog

AN E-MAIL APPEARS IN MY IN-BOX FROM ERIN, WITH THE subject line A UNIQUE DOG. Right away I'm skeptical—yet I also feel an equal degree of sympathy. We all think our dogs are unique.

On November 29, 2005, my husband David and I adopted eight-month-old Max, a male German shepherd/border collie mix, from the North Texas Humane Society. We fell in love with Max instantly, and we had him for one week before taking him back in to the Humane Society to be neutered.

The night after Max's return from surgery, Erin and David noticed that his abdomen seemed to be filling with blood. They could see the reddish-purple stain spreading beneath the skin, so they rushed him to an emergency clinic.

"Everyone thought that he had pulled the sutures out," Erin said. But the diagnosis was something much worse. The next morning, Max was still bleeding. He was diagnosed as a hemophiliac, rated moderate to severe, with a 2 percent clotting factor.

"The only time I'd heard of it was in the eighties with Ryan White, who died of AIDS from a transfusion," Erin admits to me on the phone. She went to her local library and found only one book on the subject in the entire library system. Hemophilia is an extremely rare genetic disorder carried on the X chromosome. The condition impedes the clotting ability of the blood. In a normal system, the blood forms clots to stop a wound from bleeding and allow the healing to begin. Max's hemophilia slows this process to a dangerously slow pace. Unchecked, even a small bruise will continue bleeding for as long as sixteen hours before any significant clotting might begin.

Max had been in their house at that point for a week and a day, and now they knew he had a condition for which there was no cure. Humans suffering from hemophilia can receive injections of a drug that supplements the clotting factors of their blood. If they are lucky, they have health insurance that will cover this. There is no such insurance coverage for a dog. Instead, each time Max has an accident, it requires a transfusion which costs about $700 a pop. The transfusions provide the clotting factor that he lacks. Even this process is more complicated than it is in humans. Although dogs have blood types, it doesn't work the same way as matching human blood types, so allergic reactions may occur.

This is more than most people bargain for when they adopt a pet. Erin and David had already bonded with Max. "From the time I decide to get an animal," Erin says, "that's it."

Erin and David thought the worst was over. Now that they knew what the problem was, they just needed to be careful with him. But being careful with a large, happy, courageous puppy is easier said than done. Max ran in the country. Max chased the cats. They wanted to allow him some freedom, but freedom generated bruises, and the bruises turned into hematomas as the injured area continued to fill with blood. Four months after his neuter surgery, Max was in the hospital again, this time with a hematoma six inches long that protruded three inches from the buildup of blood. An additional problem is that even with the transfusions, there is a chance that concurrent injuries will not heal. Because the coagulants focus on the first injury, there's nothing in reserve for a second bump.

It would be easy to understand a person who felt that this was a little more than they could take on, but what can we say about the people who remain committed to an animal with such a demanding condition? The cost of transfusions in Max's first year with Erin and David was over seven thousand dollars, enough to care for countless other pets. In fact, before his adoption, Max had been tagged to be euthanized, not because of his undiagnosed blood problem, but because he had a cold. That's how overcrowded the shelter was.

What exactly is it that makes some people see some animals as hopelessly demanding, while others see them as something we might term *unique*?

Look around at my own household.

Brando had such severe separation anxiety, even at four months old, that he became hysterical when the shelter staff came to feed the dogs and then left. When it was time for walks, he didn't want to go any farther than the door to the sidewalk. After I adopted him, he developed obsessive bonds with various people in the neighborhood, throwing himself down onto the street on the spot where they had stood a few days earlier. This isn't normal. And it isn't easily dealt with. While some people think that separation anxiety is a response to abandonment, in extreme cases like this, it would seem to be a brain dysfunction along the lines of obsessive-compulsive behavior in humans. It might be dormant for a while before surfacing in response to an environmental trigger, but either you have it or you don't.

Sula has separation issues as well. And, like Brando, she was a runaway when she was young. It seems logical that their runaway behavior came from the same obsessive-compulsive impulse that now makes them want me—and everyone else— to stay put.

But separation anxiety is the least of Sula's health problems. As a puppy she had two surgeries on her face, was treated for heartworm, blood diseases, recurrent digestive problems, and cysts. And that was just during her first year with me. Certainly, if she had found her way to a shelter rather than my front porch, she would have been put down.

Zephyr is little Miss Normal, except for her prey drive. She chases leaves and butterflies, and shadows of butterflies and bugs. Everyone in the park makes fun of her. On the street she occasionally tries to jump in front of the bus. "She's obviously so unhappy with you that she's trying to kill herself," one of my friends jokes.

So, does it make sense to save Max, at such great expense? I know at least one animal shelter professional who would say emphatically that it does not. I'll call her Madame X. "Is it fair to the animal?" Madame X would ask. "Or are we keeping him going to feed our own emotional state, without regard to the animal's comfort in the end?"

It's one of the curious paradoxes of the shelter world that those rare people who draw sizable salaries for their work are simultaneously the most likely to lecture about selflessness. After hearing about Brando's lengthy battle with separation anxiety, Madame X spoke with me about the possibility that he should be re-homed. Brando was on the other side of the door, whining, because, of course, he knew that we were there.

"You do realize that whining isn't normal, don't you?" she asked.

And I wondered, *Has she been listening to anything I've said?*

Madame X, by the way, is looking for another dog to add to her own collection. She'd like a male pit bull, but he must be completely passive and not focused on food, so Madame X won't have to worry about managing the aggressive female dog she keeps unsupervised at home. One wonders if she realizes that this isn't "normal."

So, does it make sense to save a unique dog? Does it matter in the end whether everything we do makes sense? While there are those who shake their fingers in disgust at people who share an emotional bond with their pets, most of us realize that what we do for our dogs is not a selfless act, and it doesn't have to be. We're returning a favor they've done for us, for all the ways they keep us in check. The Delta Society, which studies the benefits of human-animal interaction, reports that people who care for pets experience lower levels of blood pressure, cholesterol, hypertension, and illness. And there's nothing wrong with that.

• • •

After the enormous hematoma in March of 2006, Erin and Max enrolled together in a training program to certify Max as a therapy dog. Erin thinks he has a lot to offer by visiting nursing homes, hospitals, and schools. There is a lot of comfort to be found in the compassion of an animal, but even more if patients have a sense that the dog really knows what they are going through.

The following summer, Max attended the Texas Central Hemophilia Foundation Bowl-A-Thon. Even some of the adults were stunned. One man said, "I've never met a dog with my condition." Max's paw prints joined the children's handprints on a mural that was auctioned off at the end of the event.

That December Erin began sending out her "Unique Dog" e-mails to anyone she could think of who might help. And that is how she met Dr. Jean Dobbs, who runs Hemopet, the first private, nonprofit canine blood bank, located in California. There, with 125 retired greyhounds providing the universal canine blood type (the equivalent of human blood type O), she is able to supply over two thousand animal medical centers around the world. If human hemophilia is rare, the canine variety is rarer. Dr. Dobbs was able to prescribe a treatment for Max that uses cryoprecipitate, a single component of whole plasma. So now Max's treatments run at half the cost—just $300 to $400 each.

Loving a dog—or a person—doesn't mean that there aren't times when we need to put our feelings aside. And that is perhaps the one element of our relationships with dogs that makes our feelings so intense. We take them in knowing there will come a time when we will need to be with them, and support them, when it is time for them to die.

When you love an animal who has a chronic or systemic problem, your entire relationship seems to tread that fine, indistinct line each day: How much farther will you go together, and when will you know that it is time? In her essay "You and Me, Breathing" (which appears in the anthology *Dog Culture*), Annie Bruno describes the intense bond she felt with Seamus, a dog who suffered from epilepsy. "To most people it seemed like an extreme sacrifice," she writes. "Dogs were not people, they either said or implied . . . We didn't need anyone to understand why. Besides, I loved him, and this disease didn't seem worthy of taking his life. I did what I would do for anyone that I loved."

Meanwhile, Max is working out on a treadmill at home and skipping the park. The cats are staying out of his way, and he has a new housemate, a red heeler named Dobby, to keep him company.

"The whole journey with Max has led me to lots of interesting connections," Erin says.

Mine is a totally unscientific sample, but I've never heard anyone say that the worst mistake of their life was getting a dog. What they say instead is this: *I can't imagine what my life was like before . . . Having a dog has made me a more responsible person . . . Needless to say, he's the love of my life . . . I look at everything in a different way now . . .*

Our dogs connect us.

Dear Mr. Foster,

It was 1990. We had just put down our first dog, acquired five years before when we got married. Her name was Abby, a cocker spaniel. Our vet, Daniel Leiman, from Cherry Street in Brooklyn, called and said, "I have the perfect dog for you!"

So I piled our three sons—at the time they were five, four, and three months old—into our Dodge Caravan with the wood on the sides and drove down to a place called BARC. There Dr. Leiman introduced us to a Lab/Newfie mix named Rocket. Rocket was a pure black, six-month-old "puppy" who already weighed sixty pounds. Dr. Leiman said, "Try him for a week and see how it goes."

Once we got home to Woodhaven, I walked him around the house and then locked him in the hallway, as I was sure that this dog was going to eat one of our children.

Husband came home that night. I had told him I was just going to "look" at the dog. Hah! Husband knows me better than I do.

Rocket proceeded to follow him around the house, and when they went into the bedroom, Rocket jumped up on our bed and splayed himself for all the world to see. Husband fell in love!

I, in the meantime, was trying to figure out how to tell Dr. Leiman that this would never work, as I was terrified of this dog, and our house was too little for a huge dog like that.

Long story short . . .

We moved to a bigger house in Little Neck, Queens, and Rocket, since renamed "Ben," died on April 16, 2003, at precisely 6:00 p.m. I have clippings of his fur in a special box.

Four months after we lost the best dog in the world, we adopted a three-year-old Saint Bernard (don't ask!!) named Nick, who had spent the first years of his life living outside. After a week I knew that this wouldn't work, as I could not stand the "Beethoven-like" shaking of the drool. However, to quote a writer I recently discovered, "After several days . . . I couldn't stand the idea of him living with someone other than me."

Three years later, I am sitting here at my computer and Nicky is comfortably keeping my feet warm and slimy.

In between Abby, Ben, and Nicky, there have been Oscar, Cindy, Gypsy, Sara, Bella, and a host of other dogs that never actually had a name. Some stayed for a month, some for a day, and some for just a few hours until I found them a new home.

Once I even "dog-napped" a pit bull puppy that I kept finding on the street and putting back in the person's backyard. "Oh my goodness, how did she get loose again?" Well, lady, you let her loose just one time too many and now she lives with a friend in upstate New York.

Thank you, Mr. Foster, for the good that you did in writing this book. Thanks for reminding me that it has been a while since I have made a donation to BARC. And thanks for making all of my husband's groans of "Oh no, not again" every time he came home to a new furball worth the time and money!

Warmest thanks,
Rovena
Little Neck, New York

the odd
couples

BEING THE YOUNGEST IN A FAMILY IS HARD WORK: YOU TEND
to come last in everything, and at the same time, your older
siblings seem to think you get too much attention. Just ask
my pit bull Sula.

So it was quite a thrill a few years ago when my sister decided to get a family dog. For once, she was following *me*.
What appealed to me wasn't just the idea that she would be
coming to me with questions, since I finally knew more about
something than she did; I was also relieved to know that
someone else in the family would be sending out photos and
updates about a dog. And soon after her, my brother in Los
Angeles inherited an abandoned Chihuahua.

My sister, Becky, brought her two sons with her to the
shelter to pick out their dog. She steered them carefully to
something small. They already had two cats at home. As far as
she was concerned, there was no need for something big. Of
course, Vonn and Ryne had other ideas. They stood in front of
Rocky's cage and said, "We were thinking something like this."

Rocky was an adult dog. He was large and fluffy. The label on the cage said GERMAN SHEPHERD, AKITA, AND CHOW MIX. And that was probably one of the reasons he was there so long; not a good family mix. Rocky and his brother Rufus had been outdoor dogs; Rufus had been lucky enough to find a home already. They visited Rocky four times before finally taking him home. For the first year, Rocky was fine, but a little bit of a cold fish. It was as if he was trying to figure out his place in the house. He didn't play with toys. He didn't bark. He just was.

One afternoon Vonn returned from a visit to the farm with a new kitten, a little, white, one-eyed thing named Wink. She was a mess, and while she recovered from being a farm cat, Rocky sat with her and licked her. And put his entire mouth around her. "It was kind of like when a baby is so cute, you just want to squeeze it till it pops," my sister said. Every time Rocky returned home from a walk, or a soccer game watching the kids, he felt the need to race through the house and locate his Wink. And lick her.

In the summer Rocky sits out on the deck, catching bees with his mouth and spitting them dead out onto the deck. And hidden video has documented this: When Vonn practices piano, if no one else is watching, Rocky sits at his side and sings—loudly, horribly, but with conviction—for the duration of each piece.

My sister is the village council president of Pinckney, Michigan, so when I visited last year, it was big news. A local reporter interviewed us about our family dogs, and all of the pets we'd had growing up: the cats, our Samoyed, Becky's snakes, my brother's chipmunk, the hermit crabs, the tanks of fish. We posed together with Rocky on the deck and looked at each other, with a secret family look. *This is kind of silly*, the look said. Beck had arranged for me to visit the local library, so once the photo op was over, off we went.

We have a collective memory, and the interview that day revived bits and pieces of our animal past that we might not have remembered on our own. Like our adoption of two kittens in the early 1970s. We named the male calico Berlioz and the white female Marie, after the kittens from the movie *The Aristocats*. Our Samoyed, Samantha, tried to adopt them, but they were terrified of her. They ran instead to Sadie, a black cat still so feral she attacked me on the way to breakfast every morning. Eventually, Marie warmed up to Sam, who must have seemed like a giant, mountainous version of herself. They would lie together, and Marie would climb on top of Sam's sleeping body, blending in completely. At night the two of them would curl up together in Sam's metal crate, but during the day, as she got older, Marie ran free through the neighborhood. And that is how she got hit by a car.

Sam never slept in her crate again.

There was a brindle pit bull waiting for me at the Pinckney Public Library. Her name was Rose, and as people began circling around her, her butt wiggled so hard that there was nothing she could do to keep from peeing on the floor a little before being escorted by her owner, Lola, back out to the car where she waited until the event was finished. Rocky was with me, in training for our elementary school tour the following day, where I'd read from the book, and he would get petted while we talked about how to interact with a dog that isn't yours.

Lola said, "I have a story I wanted to tell you." She thought I'd understand, and I did.

She showed me a picture of Roxy, the first of her pit bulls. Roxy was a girl descended from a champion bloodline, and belonged to Lola's brother until a car hit her one day, leaving one front leg paralyzed and the other badly fractured. Lola's brother didn't have the money for the necessary surgeries, including the amputation of one leg, and the vet suggested that she be put to sleep. Instead, Lola and her mother paid for the surgeries, and a three-legged Roxy moved into their mother's house to stay. But whenever Roxy came to visit Lola, she lingered and loitered and made it clear she thought this was the place she belonged. So eventually she moved from brother to mother to sister, and that is where she stayed.

Lola lived in the country with her boyfriend, so there was a lot of room to roam around. They took walks together in the large, open field behind the house. One day Lola stopped to get eggs at a local farm.

"Come here," the farmer said. "I want to show you something." A new litter of piglets was nursing at their mother in the barn. Off to one side there was a tiny little piglet sitting alone. "What about him?" Lola said.

"That's the runt," she was told. "He'll be dead in a few days."

Lola returned to her home with the eggs and little Pee-Wee in a cardboard box. "Honey," she said, "I've brought you a son."

Pit bulls have a history with hogs, and it isn't a particularly good one. Pit bulls, in addition to being used to corner bulls in a pit, have also been (and in some places, still are) used to hunt down wild hogs. It's not a pleasant scene.

Roxy saw PeeWee and immediately took him under her wing. Or her paw, as the case may be. They were inseparable. They spent afternoons sitting side by side on the deck of the house. When Roxy napped in the sun, PeeWee stretched out behind her, pressing gently against her back. They took walks together in the field. PeeWee watched Roxy and followed her cues. He learned to sit for a treat. He mastered climbing stairs. He understood the importance of staying together in a pack. When Lola and her boyfriend got married, Roxy danced with the guests while PeeWee drank beer and passed out. "He really liked beer," Lola said.

As PeeWee got older—eventually reaching about 700 pounds—there was some negotiation. Roxy had no patience for him when he tried to steal her dog food. She had even less when he playfully charged her in the yard. "He was a prankster," Lola said. PeeWee would run straight to her, then stop on a dime and poke her with his snout. Roxy was already middle-aged when she adopted him. She was an old dog with a young hog. Still, he and Roxy began wandering a little farther away on their walks. They stopped traffic sitting together along the road. Sometimes PeeWee went out on his own. Lola returned home to find a stray dog citation pinned to the door of the house, but the word DOG was crossed out and PIG was handwritten in its place.

PeeWee moved into a pen. Roxy could go visit him, and he talked to her, in pig sounds, through the fence. And they would walk together, with Lola, through the field in the back. Sometimes Lola would find other animals sitting with PeeWee in Roxy's place: birds, raccoons, snapping turtles.

Lola has pictures: of Roxy and young PeeWee sitting on the deck, of the pit bull and the giant pig begging together for treats. She can remember every date. Roxy was born on September 25, 1989. She came to live with her in the fall of 1997. PeeWee moved in during June of 1998. When Rose, the second pit bull, arrived, PeeWee tried to bond with her too, but she was frightened of the giant pig. She had seen how he played rough with Roxy. PeeWee didn't mind; he still got excited every time he saw her.

Roxy died of cancer on December 18, 2002. "It hit him hard," Lola said. They carried Roxy's body from the house to bury her in the yard. PeeWee ran to the opposite side of his pen and hid.

"I learned so much from them," Lola said.

PeeWee lived another four years without Roxy. He died on March 3, 2007. For the last week of his life, he never got up on his feet, so Lola went out to sit with him in his pen. Rose went with her and sat with him, leaning gently against his back, even though she'd never really liked him that much.

It must have reminded PeeWee of the old days, sitting out on the deck. When Roxy was next to him. And everything was understood.

Dear Ken,

Your book broke my heart, but gave me the courage to go sign up to help at our local shelter. I got my first dog two years ago (three months after Opus, we got Milo Bloom), two basenjis that wormed their way into my heart. How did I become the kind of dog person I used to mock?

I am terrified to work at a shelter where they kill animals, but figure if I don't try and help socialize these guys, they might not get adopted. Until I got a dog, I didn't really notice how poorly they get treated. I have six crates at home. Two for the car, two for bedtime, and two in the basement in case of a tornado! Oy vey!

Best of luck to you.
Mari and her backseat buckaroos
(stuck in Topeka, Kansas
Missing Iowa City)

the vegans
in new york

A GROUP OF VEGANS HAD INVITED ME TO NEW YORK, AND I was nervous about meeting them. They had interviewed me for a wonderful story about pit bulls in their magazine *Satya*, and then they had offered to throw a party for me, and my book, as a fund-raiser for Robert at Social Tees. There would be a reading at Blue Stockings bookstore, followed by a Q and A, followed by a party with vegan wine and vegan cake and hosted at a vegan shoe store called Moo Shoes. I hadn't even realized there could be such a thing as vegan shoes, and I was worried about what would happen when they found out that I wasn't even a vegetarian—and still occasionally wore leather shoes.

It wasn't that I had perpetrated a deception—I hadn't claimed to be something I was not. In fact, in the final pages of my previous book, I made a point of including a reference to a lamb dinner, a point that had outraged more than a few readers. The scene occurs on the eve of Hurricane Katrina, as my friends and I are drinking wine and blithely planning a group birthday party that ultimately never occurs because of the storm. But in real life, the lamb reference had actually been more complicated. My friend Andy Young shared my birthday, and her boyfriend, Kahled, wanted to cook a lamb feast. Andy had been bordering on being a vegetarian for years, so the idea of a lamb on her birthday made her a little uncomfortable. On the other hand, she also knew that for Kahled, cooking the lamb was a gesture that meant something beyond simply making a meal. The lamb would be slaughtered following the Halal tradition; the lamb was, as we spoke of it, wandering a field somewhere just outside of New Orleans. Someone joked about whether the lamb would survive the storm, and months later, as I wrote the scene, what struck me was how strange it was that this was the conversation we would be having the day before Katrina struck, that we would be joking about the animal's fate (because none of us believed the storm was coming), and that we might be eating a lamb in a book about rescuing animals.

One reader e-mailed me with concern. You were supposed to be surprised, I explained. That's why I left the line in. "I'm glad you noticed that," I wrote.

But I wasn't sure I was prepared to face a whole roomful of vegans. What if they asked the question? What if it became confrontational? Finally, I asked via the safety of e-mail—is it going to be a problem that I'm not vegan? Apparently this was somewhat hilarious. "Of course not," was the reply.

After the reading, we headed to Moo Shoes, where there was a crowd of people already wolfing down vegan cupcakes and wine. I wandered the edges of the crowd, examining the amazing shoes and wishing I could afford a pair. At this point, a woman approached me and introduced herself.

"Ingrid sent me," she said. "She's worried about you and wanted to make sure you are okay." Ingrid is Ingrid Newkirk of PETA, and we had exchanged a number of e-mails when *The Dogs Who Found Me* came out, because I had outed PETA as endorsing breed bans and the euthanizing of all pit bulls. Now she was worried about me.

"Why?" I asked.

"Because when she offered to send you dog food, you never wrote back."

How do I explain this, I thought, and decided to simply tell the truth. "Her e-mails were getting so crazy that I decided I needed to cut it off." She had, indeed, offered to send me dog food, but only after first challenging me to compare checking accounts when I expressed my concern that she and PETA used the image of pit bulls to raise money while simultaneously condemning them to death. In the midst of the party, I told her representative, "Obviously we don't need to agree on everything, but I have a real issue with the decision to continue using pit bull photos to raise money while at the same time misrepresenting them with made-up facts."

"But we know that pit bulls are involved in 99 percent of all abuse cases," she said.

The number was absurd.

"We know it because of the phone calls we receive," she explained.

"You know that isn't true," I said. "And even if it was, that only suggests something about the people involved, not the dogs." Like many people who support breed bans, the people at PETA support their position with a number of assumptions that would fail any freshman course in logic. If many criminals own pit bulls, then banning pit bulls will diminish crime is one popular line of thinking.

"Let's not talk about the things we don't agree on," she said.

"As long as we don't agree on this, I'm going to keep talking about it," I said. "Tell Ingrid I said hello," I added, thinking of the old cartoon in which the wolf and the sheepdog walk to and from work every day exchanging pleasantries before getting down to business.

"Gee," a stranger asked me facetiously, "what were you two talking about?"

One of the *Satya* editors said, "We're buying dinner for you if you're hungry."

I was starving.

"But it will be a vegan dinner. Is that okay?"

"I've eaten vegan meals before," I said, and she seemed surprised. I continued, "I like good food, it doesn't have to be meat and dairy." I paused. "So it is kind of strange that I still eat it."

"Yes," she said. "I was wondering about that when I read your book."

We walked to the restaurant in a large group, many of whom took a moment to ask me what I might be anticipating about the vegan experience we were about to share. I was beginning to feel like a social experiment. It didn't seem like such a big deal to me that I was about to eat vegan, but their level of curiosity seemed on a par with what you might see if a vegetarian was about to eat his first steak.

"So," I said, trying to change the subject, "what do you feed your dogs?"

"That's a real problem," one of them admitted. Soon everyone was chiming in with their own stories. When you respect animals so much that you won't wear leather or eat an egg, what do you do with a carnivorous pet? This is easier to negotiate with dogs, who can survive on a vegetarian diet. Sula, with her digestive issues, was a vegetarian pit bull for about six months, until she discovered that she was the only vegetarian in the house. (Zephyr, on the other hand, is so opposed to vegetarian kibble that when one stray piece landed in her bowl, she managed to eat around it for weeks.) Cats, on the other hand, cannot survive on a completely vegan diet, and many have sustained systemic damage from their owners' attempts to convert them. Their higher protein consumption is one of the things that makes cat food—and the poop it produces—irresistible to some dogs.

I ordered the vegan paella, which was delicious, yet I still couldn't help wondering why vegan meals take their names from meals that are defined by the presence of meat (or in this case, fish). Throughout the meal, vegans shouted down the long table to ask what I thought of the food. And the more they asked, the more I had the urge to be less enthusiastic. But

I couldn't do it. The meal—and their company—was the best I'd had in weeks.

So, why am I not a vegan? Does it have something to do with being a lazy, untalented chef? At the very least, vegan cooking requires a lot of assembly. Yet before you even get to that point, it requires access to ingredients. In New York, there is easy access to everything. At home in New Orleans, we still have trouble accessing basic groceries two years after the storm. But I still have to admit that I know other New Orleanians who manage to do it.

• • •

The following spring, I drove across the Mississippi River for an Easter brunch, a guest of one of those sprawling New Orleans families that no one can avoid becoming absorbed in— and you wouldn't want to avoid it either, unless you have something against enormous holiday meals. Once the egg hunt had wound down, the adults settled around the dining room table while the kids sat in the kitchen and two dogs wandered back and forth between the two rooms, waiting for scraps. We passed platters of scrambled eggs, bacon, sausage, and lamb. Someone asked about my book, and I talked about all of the people I had met in the past year, and how people are surprised that I still eat meat.

And somehow that led to the story of PeeWee, the pig who was raised by the pit bull in Michigan—how the pig loved that dog.

"I didn't realize they were capable of having those kinds of feelings," one of the other guests said.

"More than anything else, PeeWee has been making me rethink my position," I admitted. "I don't think I would be able to eat pork at all if I thought about the animal when I saw it on a plate. But it's still kind of abstract. I don't immediately think of bacon as being an animal."

From the head of the table, the matriarch said, "So if you had to watch them slaughter it or do it yourself, you might feel differently?"

"I guess so, but then I'm sure I wouldn't want to eat it at all."

Everyone stopped eating for a moment, and after that silence, she said, "Well, maybe next year we won't serve meat."

Sir,

I wanted to let you know—not that my little opinion matters—but I thought The Dogs Who Found Me *was absolutely wonderful and helpful. Even though I didn't buy it, I will buy your next book. I promise. In 2001 I rescued a pit bull that looked, to me the day I found it, identical to your book cover. In fact, she and the rest of her litter were born 11 September of that year and she found me at a very odd time in my life and my career. I had recently divorced, and being in the military, I didn't know what the next few years would hold. I didn't plan to rescue her; much like your Sula and Zephyr, I think she just happened to me.*

I'm so glad she did. She was my angel and my best friend for a long time. We lived in Texas, Nevada, and South Carolina, and we also drove all around the country together. She went to several military training duty assignments with me and had an awesome time. In 2002–2003, I deployed from Nevada to Oman for the posturing and support of the war, and she stayed with my closest friend, Tawnya. Tawnya is also in the military, and when I had no choice, she kept Sjon, and when Tawyna deployed, I would take care of her two Pomeranians (plus other dogs here and there; our military family pulls together to help each other). They became very close, so much that Tawyna cried when I came home . . . not for my safe return, but because Sjon was not going to be at her side daily!

In May of 2006 I deployed again, this time to Kuwait. I hated it, but again left Sjon in the safe care of a close friend, Nadine. Even though Tawyna now lived in Massachusetts and I lived in South Carolina, another friend had become Sjon's step-mommie, and she had a wonderful time with her dog friends. Days before I returned, another friend took Sjon and his dogs on a car ride. He had errands to run and was not paying attention as closely as he should have. He accidentally left Sjon in the grass at his house and got halfway to his destination before he realized she hadn't jumped back in the truck's cab with the other dogs. He went back to get her and she had been hit by a car. She was always afraid of the street and never went near it. I can only imagine she thought if she waited next to the road, he would remember and come back to get her.

He called to tell me at 0400 on 7 October 2006 in my tent in Kuwait the day I was scheduled to come home. I was supposed to begin the twenty-hour flight home to get her that evening.

At 0600 I put a gallon of Visine in my eyes and started my out-processing so that I could start the trip back to South Carolina, even though I didn't want to go home anymore. I stopped by the makeshift library—we had to turn in a book—and on top of the book-swap (you know, take one and leave one) box was your book. It looked just like Sjon staring straight at me. And the title, The Dogs Who Found Me,

was more than a sign. I read your book before I reached U.S.
air space and I bought six more copies for Christmas presents.

   Endstate:

Since I rescued Sjon in 2001, but long before her passing, I
began to develop a business plan for my retirement (now just
four years away). I plan to open a home (NOT a kennel) for
military member's who don't have a Tawyna or a Nadine,
but need someone to love their dogs while they have to be
away from them. I don't want to encourage military people
to adopt because the lifestyle is difficult in today's military,
but sometimes dogs just find us, don't they?

   Since I read your book, I have been actively involved
with a few pet-rescue organizations in my area. I do what I
can, even if it's just to help with a fund-raiser wearing an
"Adopt-a-Bull" T-shirt or volunteer to assist in placing dogs
in the right kind of homes. I hope that I can make a differ-
ence like you have.

   Your fan,
   Laura

jimmy
is waiting

I MET JIMMY FOR THE FIRST TIME IN THE PARKING LOT OF Oakland Animal Services at the end of a very long midsummer day. I had flown in from New Orleans just a few hours earlier, and headed straight to Oakland on the BART train, dragging my luggage behind me the entire way.

"You'll want to take a cab," Martha had suggested, but as usual, I felt overly confident in my ability to navigate my way on foot, and ended up wheeling my luggage back and forth beneath the elevated highway before figuring out I was headed in the wrong direction. I finally arrived at Animal Services just before I was scheduled to speak.

Martha, one of the volunteers there, had written to me a few months earlier:

> Hi, Ken,
>
> I just finished the book—I actually heard part of the interview on *Fresh Air*. I was moved by your stories. I'm a volunteer at the Oakland Animal

Shelter here in Oakland, California, and of course, we have a majority of pit bulls. They have made me love them. I have had the privilege of fostering one for two months (after he had lived in the shelter for six months of his young life), and was able to find a great family for him. I'd love to see if there is any possibility of you coming by the shelter when you are in San Francisco. We have a nonprofit that could set up some sort of activity if you have the time.

I am looking for any way to help change the public attitude toward bullies; it breaks my heart to see how many have been mistreated and how others aren't socialized. People see the pit bulls and are afraid of them. We are able to adopt out a fair number, but I think we can do better.

Anyway, thanks again. Your book made me cry at times, and feel anxious, but in the end, it made me want to do more.

Martha

I had already committed to doing an event with the San Francisco SPCA, so it was completely reasonable to schedule something on the other side of the Bay. Yet, after going to the trouble of setting up my informal talk with volunteers, Martha wasn't able to make it to the event herself. She had a more pressing commitment: her new foster dog Jimmy was scheduled to begin classes that evening with BAD RAP, a Bay Area organization that advocates for the pit bull breed while enforcing strict training standards—not just for the dogs, but also for the people who own them. So all I got from the two of them was a quick hello and they were off. I felt a bit jealous—attending a BAD RAP training sounded far more interesting to me than listening to myself speak.

There's a huge difference in the experience of people who volunteer to take an animal into their home—through adoption or fostering—and those who volunteer in a public shelter day after day. Those volunteers have to do the hard, essential work that many of the rest of us manage to avoid. They have to deal with the reality of overcrowding and the difficult decisions involved in shelter triage. Not all of the animals will be saved, yet the volunteers are there to make a difference, in spite of the odds. I wanted to make sure that I acknowledged their contributions, because so often volunteers can feel that they are invisible.

After my talk, I toured the facilities and was impressed by what they were able to accomplish within the confines of being a public shelter. The buildings were clean, well organized, and pleasant to wander through while meeting all the cats and dogs who were waiting for another place to call home. A group of us sat out on the lawn afterwards until Martha and Jimmy showed up again. Jimmy was cute: golden-haired, eager to get attention. A typical pit bull. We made plans to meet at a restaurant, and Martha and Jimmy disappeared again. He would have to stay at home while we were out having a good time.

But Jimmy was the center of our conversation as we drank margaritas and waited for our food at a Mexican place in Alameda. Martha explained that Jimmy had come into the shelter with a broken pelvis from a hit-and-run. Yet even in that condition, he had managed to wag his tail and offer kisses to everyone, so he had been saved.

You hear stories about public shelters all the time—about the number of animals put down, about the way these decisions are made. Often if an animal is sick or of a particular breed, they get dumped into the category of "unadoptable," which means that they aren't even counted among the statistics of euthanized dogs. This is how some shelters are able to claim they only euthanize 2 percent of their animals. Jimmy would have fallen into this category at many shelters because his post-accident treatment promised to be long and costly, and there was no telling whether there would be a home waiting for him at the end.

Fortunately, some shelters are able to make exceptions, and Jimmy was an exceptional dog. Martha said it wasn't out of character for Oakland Animal Services to invest in a dog like Jimmy, because his temperament seemed so stable, even under stress. But he needed to recover in an environment that would give him the attention he deserved. Martha is a nurse practitioner; she returned to the States from Chile about ten years ago to complete her degree, and once she was done, she started volunteering at Oakland Animal Services because of her love of animals, and because she knew it was a shelter where volunteering could really make a difference.

"How was class?" I asked.

Not so good, apparently. "He cried the entire time," Martha said.

"The strangled chicken?"

Martha nodded. The strangled chicken is the high-pitched, birdlike noise made by inappropriately excited pits. Martha thought they would be tossed out, but so far, things were okay. Five weeks to go.

• • •

I returned to my own dogs in New Orleans, and didn't think about Jimmy until October, when I found myself without a hotel on the weekend of BAD RAP's annual conference. Martha met me at the airport and drove me to her place in Oakland, where she lived with her son, his wife, their golden retriever Akilies, and an enormous tank of fish.

"Jimmy will be happy to see you," Martha said, and I realized that three months had passed and Martha was still fostering him.

He and Akilies were waiting together in the kitchen when I arrived, and I headed straight for Jimmy, bent over him, and began tickling his sides. Both of the dogs were flabbergasted. In fact, I honestly believe that Akilies's jaw dropped open. "This is a first," Martha said.

"Really?" I asked. I was down on the ground already with Jimmy.

"No one runs over to greet the pit bull," she said. "They usually head straight for the golden retriever."

• • •

In the morning, I joined the dogs for their walk. Jimmy danced at my feet, lost his balance, took a moment to compose himself, and then we were off, with Akilies and Martha teamed up next to us. Walking in the Bay Area has its challenges, with lots of hills to climb up and down, and winding roads that would have lost me if I hadn't had a guide. But none of these were as challenging as the pussycat row that was located midway though the walk.

Jimmy craned his neck, looking under cars and into yards, occasionally spotting one of the cats and letting out a squeal, but he was a dog after all, and we made it through this obstacle course intact. Back in the kitchen, I had a cup of coffee while Martha prepared the dogs' bowls and had them lay in the middle of the floor for a full minute before giving them the command to go eat.

The BAD RAP conference was held at a waterfront hotel and conference center, and like most hotel conferences, there was coffee service in the registration area, a catered lunch scheduled for midday, and hotel staff buzzing back and forth, making sure the PowerPoint technology and PA system were working. I wondered what they would think the following day, when we would be joined by a delegation of actual pit bulls.

The remarkable surprise about pit bull conferences—I've now been to several—is that the people who attend are not at all what you'd expect, even after you've put aside all of the prejudices you may have had about the breed. It is almost entirely women—about 95 percent—and they are evenly split between two groups: young, tattooed, hip go-getters, and academic-looking older women, some wearing business suits. Most of the men are there with their wives or girlfriends.

The sessions that morning alternated between celebratory and grim, as the leaders of BAD RAP and their guest speakers shared stories of the clownlike behavior of the traditional, even-tempered pit bull along with horror stories of dogfighting, back-yard breeding, and abuse. With so many pit bulls abandoned to shelters, not all of them can be saved. Donna Reynolds and Tim Racer, who head the organization, told stories—with slides—about their experiences, including the painful decisions that need to be made in order to preserve the best of the breed.

They were remarkable in their honesty, and in their willingness to cry while speaking at the podium about the cases in which a young, abused pit bull didn't make it through their rigorous temperament testing. They spoke of every case, even the ones that were in their care all too briefly, using the dogs' individual names.

It's important to name them, Donna said. To give them the respect they deserve, even if in some cases, they are too fearful or too immature in their response to stimuli and need to be put to sleep in the end.

When I went on tour for *The Dogs Who Found Me*, I was startled to see the strangers gathered to wait for me at bookstores around the country. This is what you hope for on a book tour, but not what you expect. Who could they be? What I discovered, rather quickly, is that many of them were people with pit bulls at home, who had picked up the book the minute it came out because it was the first time they had seen a dog that looked like theirs on the cover of a book. I wanted to be anonymous here, so I sat quietly through all the sessions. By lunchtime, however, people were asking, "Are you . . . ?"

"Yes," I said, and quickly steered the conversation to something else. Sitting with other people who have pit bulls waiting for them at home, it is easy to find things to talk about other than my own.

• • •

Jimmy was waiting for me at Martha's house, and I got to squeeze him as much as I liked while thinking of mine, back in New Orleans. In the morning I packed my bags as Jimmy watched from the door to my room. Not wanting to overstay my welcome, I had decided to check into a room after the conference closed on Sunday. On the ride to the hotel, Martha and I continued to talk about Jimmy and what his chances were to find a home. Jimmy wasn't perfect. He was fine with Akilies, and other dogs, one on one, but in a crowd he had some dog-to-dog issues he hadn't worked through. People are reluctant to take on dogs that need to be managed, and those who are fostering them often find it hard to be sure that adoption candidates really do understand the parameters that have been set.

I considered what it would be like to spend the night without a dog in my room.

"Would it be too much trouble to stay till tomorrow?" I asked. Martha dropped me off and drove my luggage back to the house.

This was the day that we were really waiting for: A dozen pit bulls would be joining us, and, if we were lucky, we might be judged worthy of their attention. After several more sessions, covering the history of the breed, how to include children in training, and more on the issue of testing for temperament, the pageant began. The first of the dogs was an enormous blue pit, with a head like a watermelon. If we got to work with them later, that was the one I wanted. About a dozen more joined him, and the sample trainer course began. The main exercise was testing their socialization, and of course, these dogs had all been prescreened. They were graduates.

Standing in two lines, facing each other, we crossed the room, maintaining the attention and focus of our pit bull partners. This is more difficult than one might imagine, because it requires that the humans pay attention to what is going on around us. I felt a knot in my stomach. I flashed back to junior high gym class and our annual segment of instruction in folk dance. The BAD RAP leaders were at the microphone, ready to call out their instructions. I suddenly realized that we were, essentially, about to square dance. The move we were to perform was the do-si-do, but we were not required to retreat backwards.

I had originally planned to sit passively on the edges of the room, just observing, but suddenly, the choreographed activity seemed to be the culmination of the entire weekend. They had been evaluating us in the same way they evaluated the dogs. Were we biddable? Did we maintain eye contact? Could we demonstrate a stable temperament even while under various degrees of duress? Did we wiggle our butts when they walked into the room? (Well, maybe not that last one.) Only those of us who had demonstrated a sound sense of our place in the room would be allowed on the other end of a leash with the dogs. This all made perfect sense to me. I put my hand in the air to see if they would call me, and the next thing I knew, I was standing in line with a female dog at my side.

Reluctantly at my side. At first I wondered if it was my own prejudice that was poisoning our interactions, if she perhaps sensed my disappointment at being paired with her, instead of one of the brawny, athletic, big-headed dogs I'd been admiring all afternoon.

"She's very shy around men," someone told me, and then I understood. One of the staff came over to reposition my two-handed grip on the leash. We crossed the room, and my dance partner spotted her female foster mom observing along the sidelines, let out a wail, and headed for her. A staff member showed me how to guide the dog back around by stepping toward her, essentially nudging her to our goal destination. I felt as if I'd never had a leash in my hands. Finally, we were released, and I rushed to hide against the wall of the conference room. Just like junior high gym class.

I watched as the final round of pairs was gathered, and one dog took a squat and did his business in the middle of the room as his handler stood oblivious. The staff ran out with towels and spray bottles and disinfectant, and the offense was immediately addressed. At least that hadn't happened to me.

•••

Jimmy was waiting when I returned, and he flopped over for a belly rub. Martha's son and daughter-in-law were in the kitchen, cooking and drinking wine. I was exhausted.

In the morning I would see the last of Jimmy—at least until I had some excuse to return. I wondered if Martha would be able to give him up, now that they had been through so much together: the surgeries, the physical therapy, the BAD RAP training.

"Oh," she said, when I asked. "He's here for good, if that's what happens." This is the difficult part of fostering a dog: In the end, it is part of your duty to give him up to his permanent home, while at the same time remaining sufficiently committed to keeping him indefinitely, if need be. This is where foster owners become permanent owners. This is how Sula became Sula Foster, setting up residence permanently in my house and cutting short my run of taking in dogs on my own.

• • •

When I e-mailed Martha for an update four months later, I didn't hear anything back right away, and I worried that something had gone wrong. But Jimmy was fine:

> Hi Ken,
>
> I'm on vacation, but Jimmy has a new home with a woman about an hour away from Oakland. He was adopted at the beginning of January and is doing super well so far—although I've been away for two weeks and don't have any updates. She fell in love with him, and he's doing well with her fourteen-year-old fox terrier (except that he wants to play and the other dog is a little too old for him). When I went to visit, he was a little show-off in a leather bomber jacket, using a doggy door and jumping up on the couch. I am so happy for him— although I miss him a lot, cried after he left . . . He lived with me for eight months!! I'll send an updated picture of him when I get back. I told her that you want to include him in your next book, and she is totally up for it. How are things going for you??
>
> Martha

Ken—

I was at the book signing at BARC this weekend. (I was the guy with the umbrella that had never had a book signed before . . . OK, that probably describes half of the people there that day.)

Anyway, I read the book cover to cover tonight—couldn't put it down. Sending it to Mom next; luckily there were only a few tear-jerking parts, so she won't be too mad. (She and I are both suckers for animal stories.)

Some of your stories really reminded me of myself—especially the one about the neighbor's dog. In a slightly different version of that, I found a dog wandering around on my lawn in college. Had a rabies tag, but no owner's tag. I went door to door, trying to find who she belonged to, to no avail. Eventually I dropped her off at a local groomer, in case maybe she could get the word out more or have the resources to track down the registration on the rabies tag. A few days later, the dog was back, on my neighbor's lawn, with her owner. As it turns out, she had just let the dog out for a few minutes when I snatched her up to try to find her owner. For some reason it never occurred to me to ask the neighbor, as I had never even realized she had a dog in the first place. My friends still make fun of me to this day on that one.

(Something similar happened a few months ago: I saw a "stray" dog wandering around at the diner on Berry Street, and was going to pick her up and take her to BARC. None *of the patrons seemed to be claiming her. When I went to pick her up, she, of course, went running back under the legs of her owner, who apparently didn't ever hear me yelling "Does this dog belong to anyone here??")*

Good times.
Thanks for a great read. :)
—D

the beagle
who bit me

SULA WAS SITTING ON MY LAP IN A VETERINARY EMERGENCY room—more stomach problems—when it happened again. Across from us was a retired couple with a sick yellow Lab, and next to us were a couple of men with a small yapping pug. The pug kept pulling on its leash, trying to get closer to Sula, and finally one of the men barked, "I don't trust that dog."

For a moment I actually thought he was talking about the pug, who was the only one of the dogs making any move toward confrontation. Of course, he wasn't. He was talking about Sula, the pit.

"I guess you like those mean dogs," the woman said.

Sula was now flat against the floor, her legs splayed out behind her like a roast. She was smiling up at the woman.

"Does she seem mean to you?" I asked.

"Well, no."

"I still don't trust them," the man with the pug said.

The pug had a puncture in its side from a rottweiler. The rottweiler, it turned out, belonged to one of the men with the pug. The pug, I think, was his neighbor's. The yellow Lab had been abandoned by the older couple's son. I was the only person there with my own dog. The two men and the pug disappeared behind the examination door, and I heard the vet talking to them in an unusually loud voice, so everyone in the waiting area could hear.

"This isn't a bite," he said, explaining that it was too deep for there not to be any additional marks on the dog. "It's more of a stab wound," he said. The rottweiler may not have been involved at all. The men emerged from the exam room, and the larger of the two tried to hide behind a post, to avoid being attacked by Sula, who was still quietly sprawled out on the floor.

Years ago, when Brando and I were still living in New York, we began to walk uptown from the East Village to use the dog run at Madison Square Park. The park in our own neighborhood was too crowded, and Brando had grown too possessive of it, so I found that by venturing out into neighborhoods that were not our own, Brando went back to being a respectable dog.

Strangers would stop Brando and me on the street. Standing at a crowded crosswalk, businessmen would put the colleagues on the other end of their cell phones on hold. They would lean over my shoulder and ask, "What kind of dog is that?" They said it in the same manner people might inquire about the sandwich you had just ordered at a deli counter. Brando was tall and striped. He was exotic. Sometimes I could tell when foreigners behind us were talking about him; I would hear the word *giraffe*. Or I would hear one person turn to the other as they passed: "I saw a show about that dog on the Discovery channel."

Sometimes, rather than ask, people would guess.

"Is that a hyena?" This was, without a doubt, the most popular guess. It came from affluent, educated, successful, sane, city people. It was hard to find a way of saying no without being rude. It was particularly difficult since I wasn't exactly sure what he was myself. At times, the easiest answer was just to say, "Yes, he is a hyena. And I'm walking him through Manhattan on a leash."

Because Madison Park isn't in the middle of a residential neighborhood, the traffic through the run was more sporadic. There were fewer dog traffic jams, and more space to actually run. Brando and I could play fetch on one end and the other dogs didn't even think of trying to join us, although sometimes we invited them. There was a rottweiler who came every day to push a cinder block obsessively across the run; if you were in his way, he would sit staring at the block until you moved and he was able to push it again. It was all incredibly mellow.

Until . . .

One day I was sitting along the side reading a paper when I glanced up to see Brando being charged by a beagle. Brando was sitting in the middle of the run and the beagle ran up to him, barked like crazy, and retreated, only to start all over again. Each time the beagle approached him, Brando looked at the dog like he was crazy—the same kind of look

I gave crazy people on the street (the ones you can't ignore but with whom you have no intention of getting caught in conversation).

It was clear that the beagle's invisible owner was doing nothing to stop the confrontation, so I walked over to take Brando out. There was a limit to how many times he could be charged by another dog without responding, and since Brando was a big brindle dog, and the beagle was small and supposedly cute, anything that happened would be seen as Brando's fault.

The beagle grabbed the cuff of my pants and began tugging. He turned and ran away. He came back and grabbed my pants again, tearing them, ran back a few yards and started at me again. My first thought was to disregard him, as in "Ignore it and it will go away." But ignoring things does not make them go away, particularly once they have already attached themselves to you by their teeth.

It's a small dog, I thought, so I bent over to push him away with my arm. And he bit into me and began chomping up and down my arm like I was an ear of corn.

There's a feeling of helplessness, of course. And terror. And, in this case, extreme embarrassment, even in the midst of being mauled, because the beast attacking me was a charming little beagle.

Brando sat watching the whole thing, frozen, as did most of the people in the park. Eventually two faces emerged from the crowd standing along the run's perimeter: a couple screaming at the dog, but not moving. His owners.

A woman shouted from the sidewalk: "Do you want me to call the police?"

I shook my head no before I had a chance to realize that I was bleeding. I didn't want to get the dog in trouble, but perhaps more than that, I didn't want to have an official report that something bad had happened to me. Without the report, I might be able to put the whole thing out of my mind. There was blood pouring down the underside of my arm. *My blood.* I took Brando and began to exit the park. The owners of the beagle came up to me and insisted that I sit down. They would run to the drugstore for bandages. While I was waiting for them, a police officer arrived.

"Do you want to make a report?"

"No," I said. I was thinking of the dog, and what would happen to him if a report was made. I was thinking of the fact that for a year I had chosen to enter a variety of dog parks around the city, to surround myself with dozens of unleashed dogs that were strangers to me. If you spend that much time around dogs, there must be a good chance you will eventually be bitten.

"I'm going to make a report anyway," the officer said.

The owners returned, and the man spoke with the officer while the woman poured rubbing alcohol on my wounds. After profuse and quietly polite apologies, they told me, "It's been a while since he's done something like this."

A while? This had happened previously?

Brando sat next to me on the bench. I was worried that his drive to protect me might kick in. Instead, he leaned across me to kiss her when she was done.

Dog bites are nasty, nasty things, even when they aren't serious. In addition to the bites that had actually broken the skin, there were additional bruises on my arm in the shape of a dog's mouth. It feels like getting your arm slammed in a door several times—a door with teeth. One mark was particularly deep, and because I knew exactly where to look for it, I could trace it with my finger for a year or two after the event, until one day, I realized it was gone.

We didn't go back to Madison Park, but occasionally strangers stopped us on the street to say "I saw what that dog did to you."

People like to think that if they avoid a particular kind of dog, they will never be bitten, in the same way that some people assume that if they avoid certain kinds of people, they will never be victimized by crime. If you look at the statistics, you'll realize we are all far more likely to be injured by a car than attacked by a dog. In my case, the reason the dog attacked had nothing to do with his being a beagle, and everything to do with his prior history, and his owners, who had ignored the signs that there was something wrong.

Still, it's hard for me to muster the courage to greet another beagle, just as it must be difficult for a victim of a car accident to retrurn to the road.

Dear Ken,

I saw you at Dog Day and bought a copy of your book. I'm the LA/SPCA volunteer with the big goofy brindle pit (Trap Jack) who was wearing a T-shirt (hope that narrows it down). Anyway, I got a picture back that I thought you might enjoy, so I figured I'd pass it along. Also, I'll be volunteering at Barnes & Noble during one of your signings, bringing some dogs available for adoption from the shelter, so I'll see you there. :)

A side note: Trap Jack was another pit deemed "unadoptable" because of his breed and a history of abuse/neglect. I took him as my foster right before his scheduled euthanasia. Within a few days, I decided I couldn't possibly live without him (of course). My landlord at the time wouldn't allow me to keep him in the house unsupervised, so for six months I dropped him off at the LA/SPCA every morning (where he "worked" behind the front desk as the temperament-testing dog) and picked him up every evening after work while I searched for pit-friendly apartments. I finally found one, and I officially adopted Trap on move-in day, June 1, 2005. When Hurricane Katrina came, we evacuated along with another (pit bull) foster dog. Upon our return, we found that our apartment was unscathed . . . but my old apartment was completely destroyed. If I hadn't adopted Trap, I would have lost EVERYTHING. I'm convinced it was fate, and I'm thankful every day that he found me. :)

—Emily

the
chicago loop

———

I AM IN CHICAGO AND IN NEED OF A DOG. I AM STAYING
with Elizabeth and Ben, who are dogless. But I know from
reading Elizabeth's blog that her friend Megan has a mutt
named Mojo, so I put in my request. Could Mojo join me for
an interview on the noon news? A few months earlier, in San
Francisco, trying to find a dog for a photo shoot for
Newsweek, everyone I called thought I was insane. And
maybe I was—but the more press I did, the more I wanted to
focus some attention on dogs rather than myself. Then, when
my fifteen minutes were up, I would retreat to anonymity
with my own dogs, and hopefully some other dogs would end
up getting a home.

My schedule in Chicago is too frantic to make sense of,
so borrowing a dog seemed the way to go. Elizabeth had
taken care of Mojo while Megan and her boyfriend/fiancé
/eventual husband were out of town, and she had an enormous dog crush on him. Megan had posted something
about how she had intentionally found a pit bull mix after
observing how playful they were, how focused on their people.

She had grown up with hunting dogs whose focus was so intense it excluded her; this time around, she was looking for a companion dog. I hadn't met him yet, but I was already in love.

What I'd prefer is to bring on an animal that is actually still looking for a home, but in the past this has proven nearly impossible. Rescue groups can be strangely proprietary about their dogs appearing on TV, and you also have to consider the logistics of getting the dog out of their kennel and across town. Better to go with a spokesdog.

Mojo arrives at Elizabeth's house and the fun begins. After introductions, the three of us pile into Megan's car and we drive across town. Mojo is a bit of a rascal, a clown, but in the best possible way. We make it through security, then settle into a greenroom to wait for the show to begin. Mojo's a celebrity already. There are knocks at the door.

"Is this the dog?" they ask, as if they have heard all about him.

Mojo is a little unsure of things, so he settles in next to Megan on the couch. Two things occur to me: One, he should get used to being with me, quickly, since any minute now we'll be called to the set; and two, he's probably not supposed to be on the couch. "Maybe I can walk him around in the hall," I suggest, "so he won't make a fuss when we have to leave you."

"Oh, he won't make a fuss," Megan says.

"But we're going to be on TV," I remind her.

On the set, Mojo curls up at my feet. I talk about dogs, and my book, and the events that I'm doing later that day: one at Kiehl's in the afternoon, another at Quimby's that night. The camera zeros in on Mojo, as the anchor asks about pit bulls. Mojo really isn't much of a pit bull, but you can see it in the shape of his skull and in the way his eyes are set on his face. I tell the anchor that since pit bulls aren't really a breed, any dog that looks remotely like a pit would be put to sleep if they enacted a ban. Mutts like Mojo would be on the list.

Mojo, as if on cue, looks into the camera and tilts his head.

Megan and Mojo drop me off at Kiehl's, the skin care place, where I spend the afternoon watching well-dressed women arrive, seeking eye cream. They find two red-nosed pit bulls waiting to greet them instead. Nicky and Edy are littermates, now fully grown. They live at a shelter called Furry Friends, and since they've never spent a day apart, they have to be adopted as a pair. Like a house that never sells, they've had a number of offers, but they've always fallen through. On a wall near the back of the store, a bulletin board features Polaroids of all the customers' dogs, but for today, Nicky and Edy get all the attention from the staff. They've put together a travel pack of Kiehl's samples and sell signed copies of my book with the sample bag. The money goes to the dogs.

We reconvene at Quimby's bookstore for a reading that night. Elizabeth and Megan read with me. Mojo is in the audience. Nicky and Edy are there too. When I read about abandoned dogs, one of the dogs whimpers loudly enough for everyone to hear. Someone asks what I think about proposed legislation that would ban certain breeds of dogs. I talk about statistics and the factors that are involved in nearly every serious dog attack: reproductive status, tethering, training, owner responsibility. "Legislators are reluctant to address issues that involve people," I say. "It's much easier for them to blame a breed and pretend that the problem is solved. It's much easier for them to just put all the dogs to sleep."

In the middle of the sentence my voice stops working and the words are caught in my throat. I'm not talking about dogs in general anymore. I'm talking about Nicky and Edy, who are lying together on the floor at the front of the store.

"That was so emo!" Elizabeth says later. I tell her it has been happening so often I don't pay attention anymore; what's strange is that it isn't even what I'm reading that makes me cry—it's everything connected to what I'm saying. Everything that is real, and concrete. Everything, like Nicky and Edy.

We're in her dogless apartment, waiting for her husband to come home. When we first met, I didn't have a dog and Elizabeth didn't have a husband. Their home is decorated with art they've made for each other. My house is decorated with chewed-up bones and shed fur. Elizabeth took a class from me one summer in Iowa City, and now she's published two books and is teaching all over the city. Megan teaches everywhere, too, and runs a reading series. I think it would be great to live in a functioning city, but not one that is this cold.

. . .

I arrive in Iowa the next morning, exhausted. I stop by Prairie Lights early to read a magazine. In *Poets & Writers*, I see that my friend Julia Kamysz Lane has written a piece about losing all of her first editions in Katrina, and I remember that she lives in Illinois now, just outside the city, but I forgot to give her a call about coming to town. In her essay, she mentions my collection of stories among the signed editions she lost and cannot replace. Elizabeth reads the essay too, and e-mails me to ask if I have Julia's address; she wants to send her a first edition Valerie Martin that is sitting high and dry on her Chicago shelf.

That night, I read live on the radio, and it happens again. I read the end of our story—Brando, Zephyr, and I, evacuating and returning to New Orleans. I figure that since this may be my last event ever, I may as well give this section a spin. Dry mouth. Voice cracks. I drink water and begin again.

I need to stop traveling. I need to hug my dogs. I call the dogsitter to check in.

After the reading, I stop by the Pet Station downtown, to meet the stray dogs they've taken in. After hours, they open the crates and let them run free. I'm down on the floor with them as the owner fills me in on their stories. There's a sad-looking dachshund recovering from what looks to me like abdominal surgery.

She says something like "His penis was too big." It takes

a moment for this to register. "It's more common than you'd think. Their legs are so short. It becomes a problem."

No matter how many stories I hear, I can still be surprised.

• • •

Animals create unexpected connections. Dogs in particular, because they are always seeking to connect. Out of the blue I get an e-mail from another writer, Anne Calcagno:

> About five years ago, my daughter Jessie wanted to volunteer at a shelter. As she was a minor, I had to join her. I didn't know much about dogs (we had three cats). Little did I know, my life would change. I am now addicted to dogs, and the bully breeds more than any because so very many are abandoned and misunderstood.

Not only is Anne a novelist, but she also lives and teaches in Chicago, at the Art Institute. Somehow she and Elizabeth have never met.

On the phone, Anne tells me, "I must have been the worst volunteer ever known at the Evanston shelter. I thought dogs were just big cats. It didn't occur to me that they wanted social interaction." She recalls the shock of seeing a group of teenagers drop off a black and bloodied pit bull that had lost a fight. "Of course they said they had found it and didn't know whose it was." She puzzled over the numbers of abused dogs that continued to pour in. "Who has a dog for seven months but doesn't bother to feed him—for seven months?"

But eventually she couldn't ignore that there was a deeper something involved. "We volunteered every Tuesday night, sometimes more. And there were dogs that understood us. They were drawn to my daughter—and to me as her mother."

Anne had observed her daughter's compassion toward animals since the girl was two. She was keyed in on all of the neighborhood dogs around them; it was something that sprang up in her on its own. "What was really amazing in spending time together in the shelter was seeing how some of the dogs bonded immediately with my daughter and recognized what an amazing girl she was."

It was only a matter of time before they took a dog home. Jessie has moved away to college now, but Qalilah, an American Staffordshire, and Luna, a German shepherd, sleep with her younger brother each night.

Of course, Anne says, dogs are wonderful for writers. They force us out. They point out details that might otherwise be skipped. And so, Elizabeth ends up getting a dog too. From Julia. Julia and her husband drive into the city with two choices in the back of their car. It's January, and Elizabeth tacks a tantalizing bit onto the end of an e-mail, thanking me for the unusual gift of a thirty-year-old Chicago beauty pageant sash: *We met Julia Lane and her husband this morning. They brought over two dogs we might adopt—well, one or the other. Just one. But they were both great. Yay!*

Julia, ever resourceful, had added them to her e-mail list after Elizabeth sent the book. One dog was a Newfoundland/border collie, the other a Catahoula leopard dog named Rasputin. Julia e-mails me about Elizabeth and Ben and the dogs. Elizabeth e-mails me about Julia and her husband and the dogs. Everyone is sharing photos. I put in my two cents: *Catahoulas are great!* Elizabeth responds: *Yeah, he's the one we're leaning toward—he's just beautiful—but so is the other one! It's like* Sophie's Choice!

Ben and Elizabeth choose Rasputin, the Catahoula. But they veto the name. Elizabeth composes a huge list of potential names, but he becomes Percy, a rather simple name. Julia and I assume that it must be a reference to Walker Percy. What else could it be? But it turns out to be the name of the family dog Ben's folks had before he was born. In an e-mail, Elizabeth adds: *His official name, though, when he steals slippers, is Percival Fontaine Barksdale Brandt.*

The most satisfying aspect of having a perfectly reasonable, career-minded friend adopt a dog is that you get to see them go over the deep end in a wonderful and sometimes embarrassing way. For example, blog entries like this:

Originally, I told Ben I wanted a dog who would only make "this much" poop. (Picture me holding small imaginary handful of poop.) Percy's poops are considerably larger. Ben's not much into poop either, but now that he's changed our nephew's poopy diapers several times, he seems to have made the adjustment. After a walk the other day, I told Ben, "You know, with two bags and a glove, you can almost not feel the poop at all."

Or this: *Nine Reasons Why My Dog Is Awesome.* (Examples: "3. He gives hugs." "8. Sometimes he sits up in Ben's armchair and looks like a man.")

Or: A photo of the two them—Elizabeth and Percy—spooning each other in bed.

At the end of the blog post, I ask, "What about his tummy? Does it smell like corn chips?"

Elizabeth thinks I'm crazy, but later she e-mails me to confirm: *His tummy doesn't smell like corn chips, but his paws do!*

When Brando was a puppy, he went through a phase of smelling like Christmas cookies. To me, anyway. "It's so amazing," I announced to anyone who would listen. "He smells just like fresh-baked Christmas cookies!"

To everyone else he probably smelled like a dog.

Hi Ken,

I am currently on holiday in Boston from the UK, and yesterday I picked up your book, The Dogs Who Found Me. *It is such a relief to read about someone else who gets involved with animals and doesn't just walk by! People either think I'm mad or incredibly kind to stop the car and deal with waifs and strays, but I'm neither; I just can't walk by and sleep at night. It's not an option.*

I am passionate about dogs. I have four of my own (or at least they have me): three English toy terriers and one boxer/Staff cross with three legs. They are part of my family, and no other factor in my life will ever interfere with their place. I get infuriated with people who take on dogs as if they were a pair of shoes, and when they no longer fit are relegated and ignored. I certainly agree with you that in the majority of cases, it is not the dog that has problems, but the human they have the misfortune to be involved with. I am a big advocate of dogs not being a "right" for people to own, but rather a massive lifelong responsibility and a privilege.

Your story hit home with me a bit too. I got my first ETT, Bert, when he had grown too big to be a show dog. The plan was then to get a playmate for him, so along came Suzi, another ETT that had too few teeth to be a show dog. Sometime after, as I still keep in touch with Bert's breeder, I came across Belle, an ETT whose leg twisted when she stood still—another failed beauty queen! So here we were with three little dogs, who soon became a pack and scrabbled along nicely. They are not very high maintenance, just requiring good food, love, and a place as near to you as possible on the settee.

About a year ago I was watching TV and I saw Mabel limp onto the screen. It was a spot about dogs needing homes. She was a lovely-looking dog, with three legs since birth and very bouncy. I tentatively e-mailed the home she was at, then followed it with a call, all the time assuming that they would be overwhelmed with new homes for her; after all, she had three legs, and the audience's gasps and oohs and aahs must have reverberated throughout the UK. I was a bit concerned to hear there had barely been a call. This ruled out my usual theory—that there will always be plenty more people to help if you can't . . . There just aren't.

Anyway, to cut a long story short, after several visits Mabel came to live with us. Like yourself, I always want things to work out, so even though there had been a very small standoff with her and Bert at the center, and my animal behaviorist (who I asked to come with me) had said there was a tiny chance that as they were both terriers, this behavior may continue, I took her.

It has at times been the hardest work of my life. Mabel is gorgeous; she has no pretensions of being queen bee—it's just that she permanently wants to play. This is the main bone of contention between herself and any other dogs: She doesn't take no for an answer, no matter how firmly the other dog asserts this. When a dog appears boring to her, instead of backing off, she stands on her back two legs and bounces down, in order to bully them into play. This of course infuriates Bert, who has two obedient females in his harem. However, I am lucky enough to be able to look after them full-time (I write from home), so I can manage them well. In fact, all Mabel needs is for me to exercise her enough so that she doesn't feel the need to annoy the others on a regular basis. I never measure her behavior by how good/bad as a dog she is, but rather how good/bad as a carer I am being. I guess what I have learnt is that dogs can be really, really hard work, but it is nothing that can't be dealt with in a safe and loving environment. There is no greater pleasure for me than about 7:30 P.M., when my dogs have been fed and exercised and we are all slumped in front of the TV. However great my life is, it will always be that much better as long as my dogs are in it.

I enjoyed your book immensely; it has made me smile with recognition, made me warm knowing how much others can care, and moved me the way only stories about dogs can. I will be recommending it to my friends the minute I get home.

Wishing you luck in your writing and your work in protecting vulnerable dogs.

Kind regards,
Sally-Anne

in dog
years

WHEN BRANDO WAS A PUPPY, HE WOKE ME IN THE MIDDLE of the night, just to check to see if I was sleeping. In the morning, as soon as I opened my eyes, Brando would pounce on me and begin kissing. As he waited for me to get dressed to take him out in the morning, I could tell by the look on his face that he didn't understand the delay. Why didn't we both just go outside naked? His enthusiasm for everything could be a bit much.

"When will he calm down?" I asked friends with older dogs.

"About five years," one said. "Then you have until he's seven. Those are the good years."

"Two years?" I asked. It already didn't seem enough.

"But they are really good years."

I have an assignment I frequently give my students, regarding point of view. We start with a *New York Times* report about an eighty-year-old woman arrested and strip-searched for playing rap music too loudly. After reading the story—which is both true and completely crazy—they retell the story from the point of view of one of the many other characters included in the report. Many pick Harry, the woman's twenty-three-year-old cat. This is a little tricky to pull off. How much does a cat know and understand about the inner workings of the NYPD? But one student took me by surprise with her account, which focused on the reversal of the dynamic between the cat and his owner. As a kitten, Harry viewed her as an old, wise, caring woman, but now that he is several decades her senior, in cat years, she seems wild, impulsive, and immature, even at eighty.

Brando's decline came very slowly and then all at once. He grew crabby. He didn't want to walk very far. He didn't want to play with other dogs. If I tossed a ball for him, he walked a few yards in that direction before deciding he was done. Some nights he insisted on having me lift him into my bed, and on cold mornings, he didn't want to get up at all. I took the leash to the door to wait for him. "I'll leave without you," I called, and that would get him running. I chalked it up to stubbornness, until one day even that didn't do it.

I went down the street with my empty leash to get a cup of coffee and expected to find him waiting, whining, on the other side of the door when I returned. But he was still in bed. I put the pieces together, and wondered why it had taken all of these little incidents, over a period of months, for me to catch on.

When I was three, I broke my leg while playing The Three Bears with my brother and sister, running through our newly carpeted house. The doctor insisted my leg wasn't broken, but my parents knew better when I didn't crawl out of my crib on my own. And so I knew that something was seriously wrong with Brando when his separation anxiety was trumped by his arthritic hips. Following the advice of my vet, Brando began taking glucosomine, chondroitin, and MSM, purchased at the drugstore and hidden in canned food. A month later I woke up on a particularly damp morning and found Brando had chewed the fur off his left hip while lying next to me as I slept. Finally I accepted the truth:

Brando was six and a half—he had just surpassed me in dog years. If I was occasionally having trouble getting out of bed, why shouldn't he?

● ● ●

These were supposed to be our good years, and instead he was falling apart before my eyes. Brando is a big dog, with a deep chest and tall giraffe legs. He may be part great Dane, but I'll never know for sure. Large dogs don't last long. The deep chest stresses the respiratory system; the large frame stresses the hips. I try not to think about how short many Danes' lives are. Many don't make it to age ten.

"Could it be something else?" I asked our vet, who can be very patient with all of my questions.

"This is the age it happens for a dog his size," the vet said. "We can make him better, but it's expensive."

"How expensive?" I asked, adding, "I guess it doesn't

really matter how expensive it is, since whatever it is I'll do it."

"It's a series of eight injections," he explained. "But it really does work. You'll need to be prepared; he's going to be a brand-new dog."

A brand-new dog? This sounded like science fiction. The vet was talking about Adequan, an injectable form of glucosomine that not only generates a more viscous joint fluid, it also—somewhat mysteriously—regenerates previously damaged cartilage. There are few side effects. I'm suspicious of things that work without anyone knowing how they work. But it was for Brando, so I immediately said yes. After the first injection, I multiplied the fee by eight and realized what I'd really signed up for. It is a bit expensive, but not as much as getting a new hip.

The following morning, Brando did a few laps around the park, galloping with his long-legged, thoroughbred body, and finally running toward me with a delirious exhausted grin. "Be careful," I reminded him. I didn't want him to overdo it before the healing had begun.

• • •

On a quick trip back to our old neighborhood in the East Village, I kept my eye on the other dogs, Brando's former peers. It was bitter cold and the streets were clear, and I was wondering how we had ever put up with such brutal weather. Still, I managed to run into a few familiar faces. Angus, the black lab, had some grey hairs on his muzzle, but after talking to him for a few minutes, he remembered to check my pocket for treats. A few blocks away, Madonna, the rottweiler, struggled with her gait. When her owner, Josh, ducked into a store, she stood hunched slightly on the sidewalk, seeming reluctant to sit down if it meant having to get up again. In the evening, I caught up with Pavla, the Catahoula, as she walked toward Avenue D with her owner and a brindle pit bull at her side. "Do you have two now?" I called, and they turned, the brindle dog danced in front of me, while Pavla looked into the distance.

"She can't stand him," he said.

Meanwhile I was relieved. It wasn't just Brando. It wasn't just me. We were all getting older.

A few weeks later, in Charlottesville, at the Virginia Festival of the Book, I sat on a panel with David Rosenfelt, who writes thrillers and spends a lot of time with dogs. He and his wife have rescued over 4,000 dogs. The Tara Foundation is named after their deceased golden; when Tara passed away in 1993, the couple began volunteering at local shelters in Southern California. They wanted to be around dogs, but they weren't ready for another dog to take Tara's place in their home. The conditions they found in shelters inspired them to begin rescuing dogs on their own terms. At the time, they lived in an apartment that limited tenants to one dog. They kept four golden retrievers at a time, but walked them individually, telling anyone who asked that they were all the same dog.

David and his wife now focus on older dogs that have

been left behind in shelters and are unlikely to find a home. No one wants a dog past its prime, but David and his wife are galvanized by their experiences sharing their home with dogs at the end of their lives. They've moved out of the apartment, needless to say. "We always have anywhere between twenty-five to thirty-five dogs, either ten years or older, or younger but with a disability that would make them unwanted by others," David explained to the audience. We were, in fact, doing our panel at the Charlottesville Senior Center. "They have the complete run of the house, four sleep on our bed with us, and they have an open door to the outside property should they choose to use it. We have a fruit orchard, duck pond, riding area for the horses we don't have, etc., so there's plenty for them to do. Having said that, they choose to stay in the house, near us humans, 99 percent of the time."

He said it looks like a battlefield in the house—sleeping bodies strewn everywhere. They usually don't know that much about the dogs that come to them, except that their lives probably weren't that great, if they ended up in a shelter at the end. Their low energy level is a big plus, he admits, as is the fact that they are usually housetrained, and people friendly. Those are likely the skills that have allowed them to survive this long. But it is their dignity that really knocks David out. "They have a gentleness, a dignity, a gratefulness, and a good nature that is amazing considering what they have been through."

"Because their lives have not been good," he says, "we feel a need, often urgent, to make sure that they end their lives happy, safe, and loved. Because of age and health, we often don't have them for very long, and there is simply no feeling greater than to know that we have made their last months or years a significant counterpoint to what happened before."

Brando continued with his injections. At the park, he developed a fierce crush on a one-year-old border collie named Leah. Leah's energy was through the roof, in typical border collie fashion. Leah's owner threw the ball, Leah went after it, and Brando chased after Leah. If we arrived at the park and Leah was missing, Brando sought out the idle tennis ball, and flounced onto the middle of the field to wait for her, sprawled out just like Leah after a long round of fetch. At home, he began leaping over furniture, not for any particular reason—just to show that he could.

Now, in the middle of the night, I open my eyes and Brando pounces. He's been waiting for me, and just as when he was a puppy, he needs to celebrate our consciousness by licking my face. And licking and licking. He sticks his tongue in my ear and makes an unappealing slurping noise. I get up and head to the back of the house. He runs into the yard while I stay at the door, waiting for him to do his business and return. I watch as he hunts for a spot. He disappears beneath the ginger tree and begins to dig. Brando is looking for his blue ball, the one that has traveled with us for years. It's 3 A.M. and he wants to play. The girls are back inside the dark house, wondering what's gotten into him.

"Come on back inside," I call.

It is true. Brando has become young again.

Unfortunately, I am still old.

Dear Ken,

I am an animal lover. Recently I have been very involved with cats . . . catch, spay, release . . . easier said than done . . . they don't always want to be released.

Sadly, I lost my rotty in a fire in Brooklyn on January 17, 2006. It was awful, needless to say. I have been helping animals for quite awhile, but losing her (Yogi) has made helping animals even more important. I also lost a beautiful black lop-earred rabbit named Max—short for Maxine— and an eleven-year-old dwarf named Indigo, in addition to a gorgeous white long-haired guinea pig named Marshmallow. It was electrical and try as I did, I could not get to them and save them. My turtle made it out (with the firefighters help), and my cats showed up . . . with lung damage . . . but alive.

Your story spoke volumes to me, particularly your paragraph about how things change you on the inside and no one knows, really, really felt like it was written for me. Thank you.

I have a friend who writes children's books and uses a pit bull mix as his cartoon inspiration. When you have a moment you must check out his site: www.sparkyswalk.com.

Light,
~monet

children
and dogs

———

BRANDO DOESN'T HAVE A LOT OF EXPERIENCE WITH KIDS. What he does know about them is this: in New York City they would stomp their feet as we passed their stoop, because they thought it was funny to see him jump in fear. In Mississippi, they would throw rocks at him from the other side of the fence, until one day I ran after them and pretended to take their picture on my phone.

"We're not trying to be mean," the kids in New York told me, "we like your dog." "We weren't trying to hit him," the kids in Mississippi said. But, of course, they were. Where do kids learn that this is the way to treat a dog? Most likely at home. It would be a relief to think that they don't actually have a dog, or any other animal, to practice on in their own yard, but in many cases they do. Around the corner from us in Mississippi, there was a family so large it reminded me of the old woman who lived in a shoe. Half a dozen kids, all mysteriously the same size, with no parents in sight. Sula loved to kiss them on her walks, although they had a dog, too. One afternoon while we were visiting, their dog, a mutt of some kind, came running out the door. He was never kept on a leash, and they had no fence around their yard. That afternoon the poor dog's back leg was flopping in the air as he ran. It was clear the bone had been broken in half.

When I asked about it, they told me there was nothing to worry about. "He ran out in front of a car," they said. I asked if they had taken him to a vet. "He doesn't need a vet," they said. "It healed on its own."

It was difficult for me to mask my concern—not just for the dog, but the kids, too. "It healed on its own," they repeated, something that had been repeated to them by one of their invisible parents. I went home and called animal control; a few days later my house was broken into and looted while I was away with my dogs. Coincidence? Maybe.

Brando is more patient with babies, because the worst they can do is get all the attention in a room. Back in New York, Brando's dog friend Lugo lived with a baby named Milo, and aside from a few incidents of stealing Milo's socks off his feet, Brando was okay with him. One afternoon, cowering in fear from the sound of a drum concert in the public garden down the street, Brando reversed his position completely when he saw Milo was going to attend. Suddenly the noise of the drummers meant less to him than the opportunity to walk alongside Milo, who was riding on the shoulders of his father.

In New Orleans, Brando was immediately taken with Silas, who lives with his parents down the street. Silas, when we first met him, liked to sit and draw. When Silas started attending school and quickly learned to read and have opinions and ride a scooter, Brando changed his mind. Being independent meant that Silas was also unpredictable, and Brando no longer trusted him. He began to bark defensively as Silas jumped up and down or ran through the yard, and finally I had to inform Brando that he wasn't allowed to visit Silas's house again.

Shortly afterwards, Silas announced that he wanted to be Brando when he grew up. "Woof! Woof! Woof!" he yelled. "I'm Brando!"

Who was more embarrassed? Me, at the fact that my dog's bad behavior was so apparent, or Silas's parents, at their son's aspiration to become a bad dog?

In Oakland last spring, my friend Derek took me on a tour of the local dog parks with his dog Oso, an old shepherd. As we walked around the bay and Oso dashed in and around the water, Derek said, "I think we may have to find him another home."

Derek and Tara had adopted Oso at the Oakland shelter, where he'd been dropped off by his family because he was child aggressive. The shelter had been diligent in informing them of this reported problem, but Tara and Derek took him anyway. The idea of having children of their own hadn't occurred to them, and it seemed absurd that this dog would be sitting in a shelter just because he didn't like kids.

Then, as often happens, their perspective about children changed, and a baby arrived.

"What has he done?" I asked.

"Nothing, but only because we haven't allowed him to be in the position to do anything," Derek said.

"Have they ever interacted together?" I asked.

"No," he said. "We don't want to take the chance." For more than a year, they had been keeping the dog barricaded in another part of the house.

"That can't possibly work," I said. "Have they really never been in the same room? Have you tried having one of you sit with the baby while the other sits holding the dog?"

"No."

"Maybe you should consult with a behaviorist," I suggested. "I mean, maybe you are right, maybe he needs to live somewhere else, but you should make sure that's the right decision, so you don't have to wonder about it later."

Derek agreed.

A few months later, I was sitting in their kitchen with the baby in a high chair. Oso was settled at her feet, waiting for Cheerios to drop. Had they consulted someone? Was the problem solved? I wanted to know but was hesitant to bring it up. "We're still maintaining dog-child apartheid, although it's relaxed a bit," he later confessed. "Pearl's getting bigger now, and I think Oso is more accustomed to her. He'll occasionally growl if she's in his space and he doesn't like it, but there's been no more lunging or snapping, and he's actually endured being hugged by her, supervised by us, of course."

"It's still an unsatisfactory situation in a number of ways," he admitted. "Both dog and child are necessarily hampered in their movements, and Pearl's getting to the age where that's not really going to fly. Pretty soon she's going to be sleeping in a bed instead of a crib, which means we can expect her to be getting up in the middle of the night to come into our room, where Oso sleeps at the foot of the bed. We're going to have to figure out what to do about that."

• • •

Segregation and supervision aren't necessarily bad ideas, if they can be done in a way that actually makes sense. Children at play lose their sense of context in the world around them. They reach a euphoric state where they forget what they are doing or where they are or what consequences their actions might have. (When I was tiny, I once hit another kid with a croquet mallet without having any idea that it wouldn't be funny. He hit me back, and I learned my lesson.) Dogs are quite the same as children in this way, which is why dogs roughhousing with children can be a very dangerous game. It is also why my Sula is allowed to smooch children while she is on a leash, but she doesn't get to play hide-and-seek with them on her own. Two dogs can knock each other playfully to the ground. A dog knocking down a child isn't playful at all. A few years ago, the *New York Times* featured this absurd and tragic headline: "Girl, 6, is strangled as playful dog pulls scarf."

• • •

Recently I had the opportunity to talk with a group of high school students about the image of dogs in our communities.

We made a list of their adjectives to describe them; they were all negative, and nearly all suggested a threat of violence. "What's most likely," I asked them. "That a person will be killed by a dog or by lightning?" It was unanimous: our un- named victim would no doubt be attacked and killed by a dog rather than by lightning. The entire classroom was certain.

"Actually, we are all far more likely to be killed by light- ning," I informed them. Actually, five times more likely. And twenty-five times more likely to simply be struck by a light- ning bolt without being killed. This comparison may seem ab- surd, but it helps to put things in perspective among people who are convinced that there is an epidemic of deadly dog at- tacks. We all know how often someone in the community is killed by lightning because that certainly makes the news. So if a real dog attack is that unlikely, why is everyone convinced that the opposite is true?

Among fatal dog attacks between the years of 1965 and 2001, 19 percent of the victims were under the age of one, with 95 percent of these occurring when the infant was left unsupervised with a dog. The second-largest group was two-year-olds, who accounted for 11 percent of fatalities, with 87 percent of these cases involving two-year-olds left unsupervised or two-year-olds who wandered off into an- other area. Boys between the ages of one and twelve were two and a half times more likely to be the victim of a fatal dog attack than girls of the same age. How do I know all of this? Because I read it in Karen Delise's statistical study

Fatal Dog Attacks. And then I called Karen at the National Canine Research Council to talk about the whole problem of kids and dogs.

"I don't remember it being such a big deal when I was younger," I told her, and she agreed.

"When I was a girl, there were dogs that terrorized me on the way to school," Karen recalled. "They would lunge and growl and worry me, and I hated taking that walk every morning, but no one thought it was unusual or terribly dangerous. Of course, now I can't imagine anyone allowing that kind of behavior—yet there is a sense that there is more of that kind of thing going on. If you look at the numbers, however, there weren't that many incidents when I was a child—and there aren't really any more happening now. Dogs are doing what dogs always did."

In fact, in the past thirty years, the average number of dog-related fatalities remains just over twenty, in a country with a dog population of roughly seventy-three million. Karen thinks that "as we become more urbanized and as we increasingly lose touch with the natural world, our perception of what is normal canine behavior has changed. We need to accept the fact that it is unreasonable to expect our dogs to never behave aggressively—especially when we don't expect, nor are we shocked, with our own species' continuous and often horrific episodes of aggression."

Having studied dog attacks for more than seventeen years, Delise has little patience for the popular myth that there are dogs that "attack for no reason." The reason may sometimes be beyond our human powers of observation—and certainly beyond the realm of excusing the consequences of an attack—but there is always a reason, she says. She adds: "Another reason to disregard claims that dogs attack without provocation or warning is that very young children, who cannot recognize canine warning signals or understand how their behavior toward a dog may appear threatening, are the most frequent victims of severe dog attacks. Older children are much more capable of recognizing a potentially dangerous situation than a toddler is capable of, which is exactly why two-year-old children are attacked by dogs more frequently than ten-year-old children."

●　●　●

Here's a scene that has become familiar to me in every city we have lived in: A group of unsupervised children arrives at the park to chase the dogs. Sometimes they gather around Zephyr, my rottie mix, and ask, "Does she bite?"

"Only if you're a bird," I tell them.

Then, "Why won't she play with us?"

"Because you're not a bird." Brando, the hyena, stays home on these afternoons, dreaming of what it might be like to be a human boy.

Hello Mister Foster,

I am at present writing a project proposal for the government of Bhutan for pets—wild and stray animal welfare in the whole country—and I would like to use some extracts of your book in my introduction and a bit more here and there. (I must admit I am in the middle of reading it, and I am sure I am going to find more "enlightened insights" in it, very much in line with the Buddhist approach.) I have been rescuing animals for the last thirty-five years (started very early) and harassed countless vets with birds, rats, cats, dogs, etc. (I am French, and the vets in France must treat for free the animals that you rescued and don't belong to you, and I made a point of reminding them . . .)

I am an architect/geographer/vet, and I became the latter studying by myself for the last fifteen years (five in Egypt, ten in Bhutan). I now run the only real animal hospital/shelter in the country (my house, I must say), and I have helped, treated, or sterilized about fifty thousand animals to this day. From stray dogs to monkeys, pets to yaks, and for a few years now, the dogs of the crown prince and other dignitaries (and all of them received the "royal" treatment).

We are a charity (private practice of human and vet medicine is illegal in Bhutan). I am not allowed to do active fund-raising in the country (no NGO or association act as yet), so we are poor, but richer every day with dog friends and some happy "owners."

I have to go for another rescue now (some people are starting to call us when they see a bad case—they are everywhere). I have to give my proposal to the Home Minister on the 25th of September, and I would really like to quote you. You write it so much better than I would, and as a published author, it would have more weight to the eyes of the board or minister than my own prose on the subject. (I have the feeling they will find me biased.)

Please?

For the future, there are a few more quotes I'd like to use for TV campaigns, posters, etc., but that's if the project is accepted. We are so very isolated here that I wonder if this will go through. Please let me know.

In any case, thank you for being you.

Very sincerely,
Marianne

the lady and
the tiger

IN ALPHABET CITY, ON THE CORNER OF SIXTH AND C, THERE was a vacant lot surrounded by chain-link fence and filled with bicycle parts and other random pieces of metal. At the center of the lot was a small prefabricated shed. There was a crazy little man who spent each day assembling bike parts and selling them, and one night I noticed a light on in the shed and realized that he also lived there.

I lived around the corner, and when Brando moved in with me, I discovered another detail that I had been missing: the crazy man had a dog. Tigre would dash back and forth through the maze of junk, and when Brando passed with me, Tigre sat at the fence and whimpered. He was a funny-looking dog — all body with short little legs. It was as if he had been assembled from spare parts and, like Brando, he was brindle.

"Hey Brando, look at him!" I said each day, and Brando would look down the street or up at the sky, anywhere but at this dog who wanted his attention. It was very snooty of him, so I continued to walk him over every day to say hello. Brando continued staring at the sky while Tigre whined and stuck his nose through the chain-link fence to get some of the treats I was carrying in my pocket. Then Brando and I were on our way, down the street and eventually over to Avenue D, where another empty lot contained a flock of chickens. These Brando was happy to give his full attention. He stood frozen and silent, watching as they staggered around the yard aimlessly, squawking. At night, if we passed again, the chickens were gone, and Brando and I would both look at the empty lot wondering where they had gone. One night I looked up and saw them, silhouetted in the branches of a tree. I had grown up in the country, just down the road from a farm where we could pick up eggs and leave money in an unattended jar, but it wasn't until I moved to Manhattan that I learned chickens can fly.

These stops became part of our afternoon routine: the chickens, the hotdog store, the park, and Tigre in his junkyard on the way home. One day, Tigre slipped out from behind the fence in his frantic attempt to get Brando's attention. He yipped and bowed and rolled over in front of us, and Brando continued to pretend that he was invisible. I opened the gate and put Tigre back in the yard again.

"He wants to fight," the junkman said. His accent was thick and possibly French—unusual in a neighborhood where most people still spoke Spanish. Tigre was pressing his nose through the gap in the fence and wagging his tail. "He is a fighter!" his owner insisted again. I didn't have the heart to tell him that his dog had already come after us and that all he had wanted to do was play.

Eventually our routine changed, and we didn't walk by as often. One day, we passed and I realized with a start that they were gone. The lot was being emptied of all of its debris, the little shed was no longer there. One of the neighbors told me that the man had been arrested. For what, I asked.

"I think he stabbed someone," he said.

• • •

A few weeks later, as we walked north on Avenue C toward the pet shop on Fourteenth, I spotted Tigre walking on the other side of the street.

"Look who it is!" I said aloud, but, of course, Brando didn't care. My eyes followed Tigre's leash to the hand that held it, which was attached to a tall blonde woman in her late twenties. She was kind of fancy, one of the many newcomers moving into the neighborhood, in boxy, ugly new apartment complexes that had replaced our community gardens. She didn't seem like his type at all. When we caught up with her, she explained, "I was walking by when they started clearing out all that stuff, and they said I could take the dog."

There was something extraordinary, seeing him now, still the same dog really, but living a completely different life. In the mornings, we would see them together, playing fetch in the ball fields along the river, and Brando suddenly was interested, now that Tigre had a proper owner. This was a context that Brando understood, and, frankly, he was probably thinking he might be able to get some attention from the blonde as well.

"Has he been neutered yet?" I asked.

"Soon," she said.

"Maybe they'll play once that's happened," I said. Brando had issues with unneutered dogs, and although Tigre seemed to be among the older intact dogs that fell under a sort of grandfather clause to Brando's policy, we didn't want to risk it.

• • •

The next time we ran into them, Tigre was a new dog again, but it wasn't from the neuter surgery. He was sporting a big heavy cast that ran the length of one of his rear legs. He was hobbling quite contentedly along the blonde woman's side.

"He broke it in three places. There's a pin inside," she said. "I went to work one morning and he wanted to come along—so he jumped out the window."

Tigre was an old dog—you could see it in the grey hair that had settled around his mouth. He had already lived a colorful life before all of this happened.

"How much is he costing you?" I asked.

"So far? Maybe six thousand dollars?" She said it flatly, the way someone might discuss the price of a good dinner or a decent apartment, things that could be expensive but so essential that it wasn't worth complaining about the price. "I didn't really ask," she admitted, as if reading my mind.

Tigre was a junkyard dog, but now she was his.

Dear Ken,

I got Gable on 9/7/01 (four days before the attacks) at BARC, which was very close to my apartment in Williamsburg. He is a pit/Lab who was severely abused physically (and emotionally, if I do say so). I nursed him to health. About fourteen months later, after a move into the city (Upper East Side), Kira came into our lives. She is a full pit, rescued from the South Bronx by "Stray from the Heart." She was found locked in a cage too small to stand in with no water or food for several days. She finally recovered, hours from death, during the heat wave in 2002.

In 2004, we packed up and moved to Miami, Florida. The dogs could not believe their luck when now, the "dog run" was right out the back door!

The culture here is so different from New York. It is normal for people to keep their dogs outside all the time, and some don't even leash and fence them, let alone neuter them. This poses a huge problem regarding strays. For the first year I was here, I ran around like a crazy lady saving every dog I found. There were occasions when the only homes I could find for the dogs were with old rescue buddies from New York and Connecticut, and in this case I flew home with the dogs and delivered them to their new homes. I was happy to do it, but I quickly depleted my savings. I have tried volunteering with various rescue groups, but there is a total lack of awareness and organization in South Florida. I've seen horrible mistakes made by people just rushing to get rid of rescues. My guess is that these dogs ended up right back where they started.

One particular case that haunts me involves a couple that rescued a boxer pup, and then decided they didn't want her when she reached her maximum size, so they let her go in the Everglades. They said that she would be better off out there. I am not sure if they actually believe that. I cried for the poor dog for days.

I could go on and on. But really, I just wanted to let you know that I greatly appreciate everything you've done. Please send some scratches to Brando, Zephyr, and Sula from me.

Regards,
Sara

the happy
end

ON A FRIDAY AFTERNOON IN DECEMBER 2005, I RECEIVED a call on my cell phone letting me know that a group of volunteers from Ohio would be leaving the following morning with a truck full of dogs from the temporary shelter that had been set up by the Louisiana SPCA in a warehouse on the other side of the Mississippi River. There was no reason to expect the call—when you drop an animal off at a shelter, it is rare that you get a chance to follow their progress. But Lori, one of the few staff members left after the storm, knew that I would want to know what became of the little dog I'd brought at Thanksgiving, and she somehow found the time to call.

One of the benefits of cell phones is that no one knows where you are when they call, so Lori didn't know that I was sitting on the rear bumper of my van, waiting for a locksmith to show up to let me back in. I had just come out of my chiropractor's office on Royal Street in the Marigny section of New Orleans. I had just been laid off from my job. I had one question on my mind.

"Where are they taking her?"

Belmont County Animal Shelter. I wrote the name down on the back of a checkbook tucked into my pocket. It was the first time I had rescued a dog and not seen the process through to the end.

• • •

When the dogs and I returned to New Orleans, six weeks after the storm, we didn't know what to expect. I had heard alternating stories about the condition of our neighborhood: it was untouched, it was total chaos, the people were running around like madmen, the animals had taken over, it was occupied by the National Guard, they had circled the area with military barricades made from gravel and barbed wire. All of these things turned out to be true in one way or another.

I had been in touch with Mikey, the landlord, and knew that he had secured the front of my house by screwing sheets of metal to the door and windows. I bought an electric screwdriver and had it ready in the driver's seat, with the correct bit in place so that we would be able to enter the house quickly. I'm not good with tools, but I managed to remove the metal plates within minutes, and entered the house to find everything almost as we had left it.

On the TV screen, there was a frozen image of a sitcom actor's mugging face. Each of the houses was marked with a code that represented who had searched it, how many live people they had found, how many dead, how many animals.

Across the street, in a fit of early hurricane humor, someone had painted the door with TWO CATS, ONE DRAG QUEEN.

I began walking my dogs individually, because I was afraid of running into packs of wild dogs with my own pack alongside me. And there were packs, usually in the distance, running in single file across the intersection a few blocks ahead of us. Chasing cats.

On a stoop around the corner from us, I saw the dog who would become Jambalaya sitting calmly, watching the neighborhood slowly return. Like a lot of the animals, she seemed so at home with her perch that I assumed there were people with her. But that's what dogs are like, even months after being abandoned: They are certain their owner is coming home. Jambalaya was rottweiler and something else, maybe corgi, if that's possible. She was long and short, but her face was all rottie. She was timid, even fearful when she saw me walking Brando or Sula, but she eventually came around for my own rottie mix, Zephyr.

She disappeared for a while, then she came back, and finally one day, she let me catch her. I took her for coffee on Frenchmen Street before heading across the river to the shelter.

I called the shelter in Ohio to leave a message on their answering machine before she even arrived. "There's a dog coming up there," I said. "She's going to be in a book I'm writing." This was the one card I felt I might hold, if needed, to make sure she found a home.

Meanwhile, as the population in the shelter stabilized, the volunteers began working with the surviving dogs. While the majority of the dogs were moved from the outdoor tents into a renovated warehouse, the most sensitive dogs remained outside in the "rehab" tent, where they could be socialized away from the din of the other dogs' barking. Some of these dogs were so nervous that they wouldn't even come to the front of the cage when we approached. Our assignment was to read to them. Susie, one of the other volunteers, insisted they preferred Harry Potter. I brought in work submitted by my students (although my students had no idea who I was testing their work on).

Of course, the dogs that seemed comfortable enough, and who had been cleared with a temperament evaluation, were walked. While I opened the kennels and took one dog out after the other, a dog named Ethel moved forward in her cage for the first time. She sat waiting at the door to her kennel, watching me.

Ethel was a pit bull mix, so of course I'd had my eye on her from the beginning. She was a strange, muted color, all earth tones, and she had the big square head of a bully. But her intake card said she was not to be walked. She hadn't yet been evaluated. After a couple days of watching her watching me, I decided to ignore the rules and took her for a walk anyway. She went outside and lay at my feet. After a few minutes we went back inside.

A few days later she'd been officially approved for walking. Ethel loved to be near people, but she didn't seem that interested in walking, or moving very much at all. And her body was beginning to change shape. One day I asked, "Is she in heat?" There had been changes in her appearance that suggested heat. "No," I was told. "Maybe it's something else. We'll have someone look at her."

A few weeks later, she was walking funny and her belly was hanging low. "Could she be pregnant?" I asked. "No," I was told. "We'll have someone look at her."

Meanwhile, Ethel was gaining fans every day among the volunteers. All of the pit bulls were, particularly among the volunteers who had never interacted with pit bulls before. Post-Katrina there were too many of them left behind for anyone to avoid. Eventually, the other volunteers also began to wonder if Ethel was pregnant. And eventually the staff confirmed that yes, she was. There would have to be a procedure, because there was no place for a litter of puppies now.

I did the math. If they were going to do something, it had better be soon. Someone said they didn't think she was that far along. I reminded them of when she had arrived. The volunteers, including me, grew uncomfortable. The new volunteer coordinator made arrangements for Ethel to go to her own vet for the operation rather than waiting through the triage of what was still an emergency clinic at the shelter.

The volunteers debated over how much Ethel understood of her situation. "I think she knows," I said. "On some level, she knows her body is getting ready for puppies." On the day of her fasting, I gave Ethel a hug and told her everything would be okay.

A few days later Ethel was back. Charlene said that she thought it was for the best. "I don't think it was a good pregnancy for her," she said, sounding as if she was talking about a close friend. She was right. Ethel was like a new dog. She played fetch. She jumped and ran.

When I arrived at the shelter one day and discovered she had been adopted, my heart sank. Of course, this doesn't make any sense. This is the happy ending we all hope for. But then you never see them again.

It was March already and the dog who had been renamed Jambalaya was still sitting in the shelter in Ohio, waiting to find a home.

Susie e-mailed me:

Hi Ken,

My name is Susan, and I'm a volunteer at the LA/SPCA and was/still am in love with Ethel. You probably heard Ethel got adopted. I got to meet one of her owners a few weeks ago when she dropped by with Ethel, and she seems really nice and said Ethel was adjusting well. Lori gave me Ethel's address and I often ride my bike that way on the chance I may see her. Haven't yet though. She is at —— N. Rampart Street, in case you want to look for her. Just finished your book, and you noted that you live on Piety. I realized you and Ethel are in the same neighborhood and wanted to let you know where she was.

I e-mailed her back: *Are you trying to get me to stalk her?*

And then I ran outside and up the street to the address, hoping that I might catch Ethel and her new owner on their way in or out of the house. I wasn't lucky enough to catch Ethel coming or going from her new home, and I wasn't quite crazy enough to stand around waiting, so I returned home and reminded myself that she had a person to watch her now, and I needed to move on too.

• • •

But Jambalaya didn't have anyone. I checked up with her on Petfinder.com. I wrote to the shelter via e-mail. I posted her photograph on my webpage and printed it in the front pages of *The Dogs Who Found Me*. I talked about her each time I gave a public reading from my book. I called the shelter and left more messages. Finally they took the time to call me back, and I acknowledged that I was being a pain in the ass. They told me Jambalaya was fine, that everyone loved her. The staff fed her sandwiches at lunch and she was getting fat.

People were beginning to move back to New Orleans. They were beginning to adopt dogs again—some for the first time, others to replace the dogs they had lost along the way. It was possible that Jambalaya would have found a home by now if she had stayed in town. On the other hand, it was also possible that something else might have happened. The staff at the Belmont County Shelter assured me that I didn't need to worry. They would take care of her. There was no rush.

Over the summer, Coffea, a coffee shop, opened directly across from the stoop where Jambalaya had once lived, so each morning as I came and went, I was reminded of her, and of the fact that someone had left her behind, and—as far as I could tell—never come back to find her again. The tenants of the house had already changed hands multiple times, so she was a sort of ghost that only I could see.

The dog park was just around the corner. One day as I was walking to Coffea, I caught the eye of a slender, athletic, smiling dog walking toward me. It was Ethel, and at the end of the leash was her new human.

"Is that Ethel?!"

Ethel looked up at me and I bent down to receive a kiss.

"I know her," I explained. "I used to know her," I corrected myself. She seemed to have become a completely different dog.

We talked for a few minutes, but Ethel had no patience for reminiscing; she wanted to get back home and on with her day.

• • •

Months passed, and around Thanksgiving I received a card in the mail, postmarked Ohio. I slipped the card out of the envelope. Like many cards that come my way, there was a photo of a dog on the cover, a bulldog reading a book. The caption read YOU WROTE THE BOOK ON BEING NICE.

Two photographs slipped out from inside: It was Jambalaya, sitting at the shelter in Ohio, while someone read to her from my book. Written on the inside and back of the card was a note, in printing that looked suspiciously like my mother's (but was not).

Just a note and pictures from me, "Jambalaya," to show you I'm fat and sassy now. I also wanted to thank you for saving my life, but I don't think there are words that can express that. I am spoiled rotten, eating "people" food, running around after hours, and going for walks. (I will not go out when it is raining or storming because I HATE getting my feet wet.) Life is good, I am happy, but I would love a home of my own—it's been a long year and I'm tired of sleeping in a cage. If you can help me find that special place called home, I'll be waiting to hear from you. My shelter mom says I am the Queen of New Orleans and a true Southern lady, and I deserve only the best. Please feel free to keep in touch . . . She knows me best and will not let any harm come to me.

When the holidays had passed, I called her shelter mom and we talked. Jambalaya had been adopted and returned. She didn't get along with the other dog in the house, which isn't all that uncommon when a shelter dog enters a new home. Her new owners weren't interested in working out the problem, so she'd come back to the shelter.

"I think everyone's forgotten," the woman told me. "They don't care anymore." She was talking about the hurricane, the animals, and New Orleans. "I don't know how much longer they'll let me keep her there," she said.

Things didn't sound as hopeful as they had before, and the truth is that the longer a dog remains in a shelter, the harder they become to place. "People want puppies," she said.

I made her promise to call me if Jambalaya needed somewhere to go, although I wasn't sure what I could do. Still, I would do something.

• • •

Months later, the day before Mardi Gras, I received an e-mail:

> Hey, Ken.
>
> My name is Brock, and I thought that you would be interested in knowing that my girlfriend Kasey and I have submitted an application to adopt Jambalaya from the Belmont County Shelter where, as you know, she has been for the last year. Kasey has been following her since we met her a bit back, and we finally decided that we have more than enough room for her in our lives.
>
> We have two dogs right now. One, Einstein,

has been with me for years. The other, Gracie, we adopted not long back from the same shelter. We're hoping to have our application approved early this week. If everything goes well, I'll send you a picture of her in her new home once we have her.

Wishing you the best,

Brock

On a recent Saturday night, I sat alone with my computer at the Bywater BBQ, a block down the street from where Jambalaya once lived. I had bowed out of a number of plans for the evening because I had too much work to do. I had to finish this book. Yet, part of me knew that I was likely to squander my time and would regret missing the gallery openings scheduled that night.

Instead of working, I was surfing the Net. A new e-mail popped onto the screen. It was from Brock. In the weeks since his first e-mail, I had been cautiously optimistic about what I might hear. Even though I hadn't seen her in all of this time, I had a disproportionate investment in Jambalaya's life getting back on track, because we were all still waiting for our lives to get back on track, too. There was a photo attached to the message, which read:

She's doing great! We brought her home on Tuesday and so far, so good. She and our other two dogs are getting used to each other pretty quickly. The picture is horrible, but here she is at home with Kasey and me, Kasey's dog Gracie (between us), and my dog Einstein.

In the photo, her adoptive family and dogs are gathered together on the couch, and Jambalaya, with a scarf tied around her now-fat neck, is sitting in front of them, unsure of what to do. Everyone else is looking directly at the camera; they appear to be a family that often takes group portraits. Jambalaya has her face turned away from the lens, looking instead at the new family gathered behind her.

Eighteen months had passed since the storm. But for us it seemed much longer.

resources

Advocates for the Underdog
A Canadian group devoted to responsible pet ownership–
sensible dog laws. They also work to fight the broad
breed-specific legislation enacted in Ontario, as well as
transporting dogs to safety. Some have even made their
way to the U.S., where they have been trained for police
work and as service dogs.
> 5060 Tecumseh Road East
> Suite 1219
> Windsor, Ontario
> N8T 1C1
> www.advocatesfortheunderdog.com

American Society for the Prevention of Cruelty to Animals (ASPCA)
If you know any animal advocacy groups, you know this
one. Established in 1866, the ASPCA is the oldest in the
country, and (as seen on Animal Planet) works with law en-
forcement in many cities to regulate animal care standards
and abuse cases. (Note: Many people assume that their local
shelter is the SPCA, but this is not always true.)

424 East 92nd Street
New York, New York 10128
(212) 876–7700
www.aspca.org

American Temperament Test Society (ATTS)

ATTS promotes uniform temperament evaluations of pure-bred and mixed-breed dogs. The group's website features statistics on the pass–fail rate of all breeds (the American pit bull and Staffordshire terrier score the same as the golden retriever!), and information on seminars addressing the psychological components of dog training and ownership.

P.O. Box 501124
Indianapolis, Indiana 46256–1124
Phone: (317) 288–4403
E-mail: info@atts.org
www.atts.org

Animal Farm Foundation

From WWI to Petey from *The Little Rascals*, Animal Farm Foundation's mission has been to "restore the image of the American Pit Bull Terrier, and to protect him from discrimination and cruelty." Whatever your feelings may be about pit bulls, this is a great source for historic images of this American breed. Animal Farm also works throughout the country to establish fair and responsible laws regarding dangerous dogs.

P.O. Box 624
Bangall, New York 12506

Phone: (518) 398–0017; Fax: (518) 398–0737
E-mail: info@animalfarmfoundation.org
www.animalfarmfoundation.org

Animal Rescue New Orleans (ARNO)

Born out of the storm, New Orleans continues to rescue
and adopt animals from the streets of the city as well as the
surrounding, abandoned areas.

271 Plauche Street
New Orleans, Louisiana 70123
Phone: (504) 571–1900
E-mail: ar-no@cox.net
www.animalrescueneworleans.org

Bay Area Dog Lovers Responsible About Pit Bulls (BAD RAP)

A nonprofit organization devoted to rescuing stray pit bulls
and pit bull mixes, as well as providing accurate information
to the public and the media. The website includes an in-
formative section on "So You Found a Stray," as well as a
hilarious gallery of pit bulls smooching with their owners.

P.O. Box 320776
San Francisco, California 94132
www.badrap.org

Belmont County Animal Shelter

These wonderful people kept Jambalaya for nearly a year
and a half—until she found a home. Thank you!

Belmont County Animal Shelter
45244 National Road West
St. Clairsville, OH 43950
Phone: (740) 695-4708
E-mail: bcarl@1st.net
http://www.petfinder.com/shelters/OH216.html

BEST FRIENDS

Established in the early 1980s, Best Friends runs a large
animal sanctuary in Utah where more than fifteen hundred
dogs, cats, horses, and rabbits live while waiting for a
permanent home. For many of them, Best Friends is their
permanent home. The Best Friends website offers
information on training and animal care.

5001 Angel Canyon Road
Kanab, Utah 84741
(435) 644–2001
www.bestfriends.org

BROOKLYN ANIMAL RESOURCE CENTER (BARC)

Established in 1987, BARC is a nonprofit no-kill shelter that
operates on donations and income generated by its animal
grooming and supply store, BQE. This is the organization
that rescued Brando and then let him come live with me.

253 Wythe Avenue
Brooklyn, New York 11211
Phone: (718) 486–7489
E-mail: tonybarc@aol.com
www.barcshelter.org

Dag's House

Inspired by a paralyzed pit bull, Kim Dudek built Dag's House, which offers housing and fitness for special needs dogs. Along with some great resources, Dag's website offers inspiring photos of dogs on wheels.

5316 August Avenue

Marrero, Louisiana 70072

Phone: (504) 218-7271

E-mail: info@dagshouse.com

www.dagshouse.com

The Delta Society

Founded in 1977 in Portland, Oregon, the mission of this organization includes:

• Expanding awareness of the positive effect animals can have on human health and development.

• Removing barriers that prevent involvement of animals in everyday life.

• Expanding the therapeutic and service role of animals in human health, service, and education.

875 124th Ave NE, Suite 101

Bellevue, Washington 98005-2531

Phone: (425) 679–5500

(8:30 A.M.–4:30 P.M. PST, Monday–Friday)

Fax: (425) 679–5539

E-mail: info@deltasociety.org

www.deltasociety.org

The Dog Park
This easily navigated directory lists some (but not all) of the thousands of dog parks in the United States, as well as information on how to start your own, dog park etiquette, and other essentials for a socialized dog.
www.thedogpark.com

Dove Lewis Emergency Animal Hospital
This Portland, Oregon organization has a wealth of up-to-the-minute health information on its website and innovative programs in the community. One favorite: Read to the Dogs, which pairs children learning to read with dogs who love to be read to.
1945 NW Pettygrove
Portland, Oregon 97209
(Preferred mailing address)
Phone: (503) 228-7281
Fax: (503) 228-0464
www.dovelewis.org

First Run
New York City's oldest dog run, First Run is located in the East Village's Tompkins Square. Although housed on city parkland, the run is fully funded and managed by the community. The website offers information on the history of the run, resources and links to training and programming opportunities, and photos of Brando's good friend, Java.
The Friends of the First Run
503 East 6th Street, Apt. 3R
New York, New York 10009
www.firstrunfriends.org

Heartworm Society

The Heartworm Society is the best resource around for
information on the treatment and prevention of this deadly
parasite. The society's website offers an explanation of how
the life cycle of the heartworm works, as well as pages
geared specifically toward pet owners and vets. For grade
school students, there is a coloring book that teaches how
to take care of pets.

P.O. Box 667
Batavia, Illinois 60510
Fax: (630) 208–8398
E-mail: info@heartwormsociety.org
www.heartwormsociety.org

Hemopet

The first private, nonprofit canine blood bank in the
United States.

11330 Markon Drive
Garden Grove, California 92841
Phone: (714) 891–2022; Fax: (714) 891–2123
E-mail: hemopet@hotmail.com
www.hemopet.org

Jackson Friends of the Animal Shelter

Local volunteers have formed this nonprofit to work
directly with the city animal shelter to provide foster
homes and promote volunteerism and local
animal rescue.

P.O. Box 13486
Jackson, Mississippi 39236
Phone: (601) 960–1775
E-mail: threedognight@bellsouth.net
www.petfinder.org/shelters/MS01.html

Kiehl's

What does Kiehl's skin care line have to do with dogs?
Established in 1851, Kiehl's doesn't use animal testing,
and many of their stores support local animal rescue
groups through sponsorships, fund-raising, and in-store
events. Their new line of dog shampoo and conditioners
are the only bathing products that are Zephyr-approved.
www.kiehls.com

Leon County Humane Society

Operating independently of the county shelter, the Leon
County Humane Society supports an extensive fostering
program that rescues animals from area shelters and
prepares them for placement in permanent homes.

413 Timberlane Road
Tallahassee, Florida 32312
Phone: (850) 224–9193; Fax: (850) 224–5209
E–mail: info@lchs.info
www.lchs.info

Louisiana SPCA (LA/SPCA)

After losing their shelter in Hurricane Katrina, the LA/SPCA opened the first phase of a new complex in May 2007.

1700 Mardi Gras Boulevard
New Orleans, Louisiana 70114
Phone: (504) 368–5191; Fax: (504) 368–3710
www.la-spca.org

Mariah's Promise

When Denver instituted a ban on any dog that even looked like a pit bull, Mariah's Promise provided temporary shelter until responsible owners were able to move out of the city and reclaim their family pet. Mariah's Promise is located on forty-three acres of land just north of Divide, and offers sanctuary to dogs and horses. It also works with two additional organizations—The Old Dog House and Blue Lion Animal Rescue—to place older dogs and large-breed or "difficult" animals.

P.O. Box 1017
4027 County Road 5
Divide, CO 80814
Phone: (719) 687–4568
E–mail: mariahspromise@msn.com
www.mariahspromise.com

Mar Vista Animal Medical Center

This center's Pet Web Library offers clever illustrations and plain language to illustrate the more difficult aspects of pet ownership—such as "More Than You Ever Wanted to Know about Anal Sacs"—as well as entries on canine cancers, Cushing's disease, and even snail bait poisoning.

3850 Grand View Boulevard
Los Angeles, California 90066
Phone: (310) 391–6741; Fax: (310) 391–6744
www.marvistavet.com

THE McKEE PROJECT

Founded by Christine Crawford, The McKee Project is dedicated to the health of animals in Latin America. Through grants and donations, they have been addressing the stray dog problem by training vets to provide quick, efficient, and low-cost spay and neuter procedures.

176 Los Arcos • Cariari • San Jose, Costa Rica
Fax: 011 506 283 9789
E-mail: Carla@McKeeMail.org
www.mckeeproject.org

MID-AMERICA BULLY BREED RESCUE

Formerly known as Kansas Pit Bull Rescue. The website offers some great stories and wonderful examples of creative fund-raising and sponsorship of individual rescues.

P.O. Box 1
Lansing, Kansas 66043
E-mail: mabbr@mabbr.org
www.mabbr.org

Missouri Pit Bull Rescue (MPR)

MPR rescues dogs from shelters that refuse to adopt the dogs to the public. After carefully evaluating the dogs in the shelter environment, MPR volunteers foster the dogs, socialize them with children and other adults, and then find them permanent homes. Another excellent site for training tips and suggestions for all dog breeds.

> P.O. Box 520043
> Independence, Missouri 64052
> E-mail: email@mprgroup.net
> www.mprgroup.net

National Canine Research Council

The National Canine Research Council is an organization comprised of canine experts to present accurate statistics and to provide detailed information on the human and canine behavoirs which have contributed to cases of severe and fatal dog attacks. The goal of NCRC is to move beyond the current media/political hysteria associated with dog attacks and investigate and analyze the circumstances, behavoirs, and environment which resulted in an incident of severe/fatal canine agression.

> www.nationalcanineresearchcouncil.org

National Hemophilia Foundation

For more information on hemophilia.

> www.hemophilia.org

New Leash on Life (NLOL)
With volunteer organizations in both Chicago and Los
Angeles, New Leash supports the sheltering and adoption
of all types of dogs, including seniors.

www.newleash.org

Chicago:

4064 N. Lincoln Avenue #374

Chicago, Illinois 60618

Phone: (312) 458–9839

Fax: (312) 264–0296

E-mail: chicago@nlol.org

Los Angeles:

16742 Placerita Cyn. Rd.

Newhall, California 91321

Phone: (661) 255–0097 or (818) 710–9898

E-mail: info@nlol.org

No Voice Unheard
Founded by Diane Leigh and Merilee Geyer, two former
shelter workers who went on to author the book *One at a
Time: A Week in an American Animal Shelter*. No Voice Unheard is a nonprofit organization whose mission is to promote an ethic of compassion and respect for all living
beings and the planet we share, and encourage a deeper
awareness of the effects our actions have on the lives and
existence of animals, the environment, and our fellow
human beings. No Voice Unheard generates exposure,
education, advocacy, and action, using the venues of

literature, music, visual art, public events, media campaigns, publications, lectures, and exhibits.

No Voice Unheard
P. O. Box 4171
Santa Cruz, California 95063
Phone: (831) 440-9574
Fax: (831) 479-3225
E–mail: info@novoiceunheard.org
www.novoiceunheard.org

Oakland Animal Services

The people who saved Jimmy! Each year Oakland Animal Services picks up over 6,000 stray, injured, abused, aggressive, and dead animals within the City of Oakland. They also offer dog training, adoptions, and other public service programs.

1101 29th Avenue
Oakland, CA 94601
Phone (24-Hour Shelter Hotline): (510) 535–5602
Fax: (510) 535–5601
www.oaklandanimalservices.org

Petfinder

Petfinder is the mother ship of online rescue groups, providing a database of more than 7,000 shelters and organizations throughout the country. The search function allows potential pet owners to look for specific breeds, sizes, ages, or genders. Petfinder is also a terrific way of seeking information on various animal rescue organizations in your local area.

www.petfinder.com

Pit Bull Rescue Central

Pit Bull Rescue Central is perhaps the best resource on the Web. Among its extensive pages are listings of pit bulls available for adoption, breed-friendly rescue groups, information on how to care for and train a stubborn dog, and excellent information on temperament testing.

www.pbrc.net

Rescuing Unwanted Friendly Fidos (RUFF)

Pam Vandenburgh started RUFF Rescue as a pit-bull-exclusive organization, but later expanded to include all breeds. The group's specialty remains "Bully Type Breeds."

8723 North Temple Avenue
Tampa, Florida 33617
Phone: (813) 985–1269
E-mail: rdemcowgrl1@aol.com
ruff.petfinder.com

San Francisco SPCA

The SF/SPCA focuses on outreach and advocacy and works with area shelters through their state-of-the-art high-volume/low-occupancy adoption center, Maddie's.

2500 16th Street
San Francisco, CA 94103
Phone: (415) 554–3000
E–mail: publicinfo@sfspca.org
www.sfspca.org

Maddie's Pet Adoption Center
250 Florida Street
San Francisco, CA 94103
Phone: (415) 522–3500
www.sfspca.org

Social Tees
A T-shirt shop that supports the fund-raising efforts of churches, schools, and nonprofits nationwide, Social Tees also operates an animal rescue operation that specializes in rehabilitating large reptiles and placing them in schools.

124 East 4th Street
New York, New York 10003
Phone: (800) 200–7338
E-mail: info@socialteez.com
www.socialteez.com

Stray Rescue of St. Louis
Founded by Randy Grim, Stray Rescue rehabilitates and finds homes for the strays of St. Louis. Randy also works with Quentin, the "miracle dog" who survived a shelter's gas chamber. Together they campaign to replace ineffective and inhumane euthanasia with more effective measures.

1463 S. 18th Street
Saint Louis, MO 63104
Phone: (314) 771–6121
www.strayrescue.org

THE SULA FOUNDATION

Inspired by his pit bull Sula, Ken Foster recently founded this organization to fund pit bull spay/neuter programs and school programs aimed at educating children and teenagers in responsible interactions with their own dogs and those they might encounter in their neighborhoods.

P.O. Box 3780
New Orleans, LA 70117
www.sulafoundation.org

THE TRUTH ABOUT PIT BULLS

Originally part of the website for the now-defunct Furry Friends Foundation, this series of pages now stands on its own.
www.thetruthaboutpitbulls.org

VOLHARD TRAINING

Tips on training and behavior from Wendy and Jack Volhard. Their Canine Personality Profile is easy to administer and offers an eye-opening look at the distinct drives that are motivating or distracting your pet.
www.volhard.com